P9-DNP-210

The Wilderness Sampler

a tonic of great writings about the moods of nature

The Wilderness Sampler

edited by

Jean C. Vermes

STACKPOLE
BOOKS
Harrisburg, Pennsylvania

THE WILDERNESS SAMPLER

Published by
STACKPOLE BOOKS
Cameron and Kelker Streets
Harrisburg, Pa. 17105

Library of Congress Catalog Card Number 68-29594
Printed in U.S.A.

ACKNOWLEDGMENTS

Prologue from *Androcles and the Lion* by George Bernard Shaw reprinted by permission of The Public Trustee and The Society of Authors, 84 Drayton Gardens, London SW. 10, England.

"The Faith of a Naturalist" from *Accepting the Universe*, copyright 1920, by John Burroughs, reprinted by permission of the publisher, Houghton Mifflin Company.

"Two in the Great North Woods" from *Grizzlies in Their Back Yard* by Beth Day, copyright © 1956 by Beth Day, reprinted by permission of Paul R. Reynolds, Inc., 599 Fifth Avenue, New York 17, N. Y.

"The Man Who Acted as the Sun" from *Tales of the North American Indians,* edited by Stith Thompson, reprinted by permission of Harvard University Press.

"Columbus and the Vagabond Birds" by Mary Leister reprinted by permission of *National Wildlife*.

"The Kingdom of Kansas" from *Paul Bunyan* by James Stevens, copyright 1925, 1947 by Alfred A. Knopf, Inc., reprinted by permission of the publisher.

"Arctic Rendezvous" from *Under the Sea-Wind* by Rachel L. Carson, copyright 1941 by Rachel L. Carson, reprinted by permission of Oxford University Press, Inc.

"Alaskan Gold Rush" from *Fifty Years in Alaska* by Carl J. Lomen reprinted by permission of David McKay Co., Inc.

CONTENTS

PART II *Nature Transformed by Poets, Bards, and Yarn-Spinners*

PART III *Adventures into the Unknown*

PART IV *Stalkers and Fugitives of the Wilds*

PART V *The Perennial Source of Our Life*

Where you can find selections by:

INTRODUCTION

Man has been writing about nature ever since cavemen drew the first pictographs. An immense variety in mood and point of view characterizes this huge body of literature, corresponding in part to the protean variety of nature herself, but also reflecting differences in the human qualities of imagination, thought, and feeling possessed by the writers. This book collects—samples—some of the best writings from this rich treasure trove.

Raw, elemental nature has always inspired awe in the mind of man. This is quite understandable in view of the fact that such tumultuous natural phenomena as earthquakes, storms, and floods compel the homage of dread and wonder. When the power of vivid descriptive writing combines with the inherent power of such cataclysmic events, as in "Earthquake Storms" by John Muir or "Tempest" by Charles Dickens, the effect on the reader can be well-nigh overwhelming. But nature needs no violence to be impressive. Even in repose, her brooding, barren wastelands and scenes of rugged desolation sternly chasten human presumptuousness, as witness "Egdon Heath" by Thomas Hardy and "The Encantadas or Enchanted Isles (Sketch First)" by Herman Melville. Part I of this anthology therefore deals with those implacable and majestic aspects of nature which instill fear and awe in the heart of man.

Unschooled bards and learned authors have coped with this

fear and awe in various ways. Primitive peoples have often sought to make the forces of nature less mysterious and fearsome by creating mythological tales to explain natural phenomena, such as the North American Indian legend, "The Man Who Acted as the Sun." At times, rather than let themselves be intimidated by natural forces over which they had no control, men have invented stories depicting superhuman heroes victoriously battling weather and landscapes more perverse than any which nature has ever pulled out of her seemingly inexhaustible bag of tricks. The Paul Bunyan story, "The Kingdom of Kansas," part of which is included in this volume, well exemplifies such tall tales.

Nature has been transformed by the imagination of poets and other creative writers in many ways. Edgar Allan Poe in "Silence —A Fable" and Robert Browning in "Childe Roland to the Dark Tower Came," for instance, have created surrealistic landscapes of such imaginative power as to conjure up feelings of awe comparable to those aroused by the imposing scenery of wilderness itself. Not only have creative writers transfigured nature's topography in their writings, they have dealt equally imaginatively with nature's creatures. Egocentric man has had a persistent tendency to remake nature in his own image and, in particular, to endow animals with human characteristics. When writers who do this do not deceive themselves that they are describing animals as they really are or allow themselves to lapse into sentimentality, they sometimes produce such delightful works as Grahame's *The Wind in the Willows* and Shaw's Prologue from *Androcles and the Lion.* Indeed, one of the charms of the latter piece is that Shaw never allows his audience to forget the absurdity of treating a lion like a house pet, as his protagonist does.

Considering that so many great writers have painted nature not in her true colors but in the hues of imagination, Part II of this book has been devoted to more or less fanciful views of nature.

Much of the best nature writing concerns the exploration of unknown wilderness. Explorers themselves have often written the best accounts of their journeys, as may be seen by perusing "The Lewis and Clark Expedition" by Reuben Gold Thwaites, taken from the journals of the leaders of the expedition, and "Voyage to the South Pole," written by Roald Amundsen, the man who lived the adventure. Part III of this sampler consists entirely of true stories of daring exploration.

Many exciting dramas of pursuit and escape have been played against the backdrop of wilderness. Sometimes, as in Rachel Carson's "Arctic Rendezvous," birds and animals hunt each other for food. Sometimes different protagonists, man and his quarry, play the deadly game. The prey may be an animal hunted for food (Francis Parkman's "The Buffalo Chase"), for sport (Audubon's "A Racoon Hunt in Kentucky"), or the satisfaction of scientific curiosity ("Trapping an Alligator" by Ralph and Chandos Temple). Or man may relentlessly track down man, as in Theodore Roosevelt's grim narrative, "An Uncanny Tale." Part IV has been devoted to tales of pursuit and escape, both true and fictional.

Part V focuses on the inspirational aspects of nature. Man has long been accustomed to look upon virgin wilderness as a restorer of his soul and a source of solace. One of the foremost exponents of the virtues of life in the wilderness was Henry David Thoreau, whose *Walden* furnishes two excerpts for this section. In the words of Thoreau:

> What do we most want to dwell near to? Not to men surely, the depot, the post-office, the bar-room, the meeting-house, the school-house, the grocery, Beacon Hill or the Five Points, where men most congregate, but to the perennial source of our life, whence in all our experience we have found that to issue, as the willow stands near the water and sends out its roots in that direction.

But how do we overlook the myriad catastrophes which nature has visited upon man and will continue to inflict in the future? Perhaps the following passage from John Burroughs' "The Faith of a Naturalist," which concludes this volume, provides the answer:

> . . . after we have painted Nature as black as the case will allow, after we have depicted her as a savage beast, a devastating storm, a scorching desert, a consuming fire, an all-engulfing earthquake, or as war, pestilence, famine, we have only depicted her from our limited human point of view. But even from that point of view the favoring conditions of life are so many, living bodies are so adaptive, the lift of the evolutionary impulse is so unconquerable, the elemental laws and forces are so overwhelmingly on our side, that our position in the universe is still an enviable one. "Though he slay me, yet will I trust in him." Slain, I shall nourish some other form of life, and the books will still balance—not my books, but the vast ledgers of the Eternal.

PART I

Untamed Power in Repose and Action

THE ENCANTADAS or ENCHANTED ISLES

Sketch First

HERMAN MELVILLE

Herman Melville, of MOBY DICK *fame, did some equally famous sketches of the uninhabited Pacific Galápagos Islands, which he called the "Encantadas." Their volcanic scenery is far from romantic, but nature doesn't have to be conventionally beautiful to be impressive.*

Melville's first sketch, part of which is presented here, first appeared in 1854 in PUTNAM'S MAGAZINE.

Take five-and-twenty heaps of cinders dumped here and there in an outside city lot; imagine some of them magnified into mountains, and the vacant lot of the sea; and you will have a fit idea of the general aspect of the Encantadas, or Enchanted Isles. A group rather of extinct volcanoes than of isles; looking much as the world at large might, after a penal conflagration.

It is to be doubted whether any spot of earth can, in desolateness, furnish a parallel to this group. Abandoned cemeteries of long ago, old cities by piecemeal tumbling to their ruin, these are melancholy enough; but, like all else which has but once been associated with humanity, they still awaken in us some thoughts of sympathy, however sad. Hence, even the Dead Sea, along with whatever other emotions it may at times inspire, does not fail to touch in the pilgrim some of his less unpleasurable feelings.

And as for solitariness; the great forests of the north, the expanses of unnavigated waters, the Greenland ice-fields, are the profoundest of solitudes to a human observer; still the magic of their changeable tides and seasons mitigates their terror; because, though unvisited by men, those forests are visited by the

May; the remotest seas reflect familiar stars even as Lake Erie does; and in the clear air of a fine Polar day, the irradiated, azure ice shows beautifully as malachite.

But the special curse, as one may call it, of the Encantadas, that which exalts them in desolation above Idumea and the Pole, is, that to them change never comes; neither the change of seasons nor of sorrows. Cut by the Equator, they know not the autumn, and they know not spring; while already reduced to the lees of fire, ruin itself can work little more upon them. The showers refresh the deserts; but in these isles, rain never falls. Like split Syrian gourds left withering in the sun, they are cracked by an everlasting drought beneath a torrid sky. "Have mercy upon me," the wailing spirit of the Encantadas seems to cry, "and send Lazarus that he may dip the tip of his finger in water and cool my tongue, for I am tormented in this flame."

EGDON HEATH

THOMAS HARDY

Thomas Hardy's great novel, The Return of the Native, *was published in 1878. Novelists took their time in telling stories back in those days, but even then it was unusual to devote the entire first chapter of a novel solely to scenic description without any mention of the characters who were to appear in the book.*

The first chapter of this novel, reprinted here, describes Egdon Heath, a barren tract of land in southwestern England near Dorchester, Hardy's birthplace, and a part of what was in King Alfred's time the kingdom of Wessex. Hardy makes his readers feel so strongly the overpowering, chastening effect which its stark, ascetic majesty had upon the minds of those who lived near it, that the human actors in the story which follows seem almost irrelevant.

A Saturday afternoon in November was approaching the time of twilight, and the vast tract of unenclosed wild known as Egdon Heath embrowned itself moment by moment. Overhead the hollow stretch of whitish cloud shutting out the sky was as a tent which had the whole heath for its floor.

The heaven being spread with this pallid screen and the earth with the darkest vegetation, their meeting-line at the horizon was clearly marked. In such contrast the heath wore the appearance of an instalment of night which had taken up its place before its astronomical hour was come: darkness had to a great extent arrived hereon, while day stood distinct in the sky. Looking upwards, a furze-cutter would have been inclined to continue work; looking down, he would have decided to finish his faggot and go home. The distant rims of the world and of the firmament seemed to be a division in time no less than a division in matter. The face of the heath by its mere complexion added half an hour to evening; it could in like manner retard the dawn, sadden noon, anticipate the frowning of storms scarcely generated, and intensify the opacity of a moonless midnight to a cause of shaking and dread.

In fact, precisely at this transitional point of its nightly roll into darkness the great and particular glory of the Egdon waste began, and nobody could be said to understand the heath who had not been there at such a time. It could best be felt when it could not clearly be seen, its complete effect and explanation lying in this and the succeeding hours before the next dawn: then, and only then, did it tell its true tale. The spot was, indeed, a near relation of night, and when night showed itself an apparent tendency to gravitate together could be perceived in its shades and the scene. The sombre stretch of rounds and hollows seemed to rise and meet the evening gloom in pure sympathy, the heath exhaling darkness as rapidly as the heavens precipitated it. And so the obscurity in the air and the obscurity in the land closed together in a black fraternization towards which each advanced half-way.

The place became full of a watchful intentness now; for when other things sank brooding to sleep the heath appeared slowly to awake and listen. Every night its Titanic form seemed to await something; but it had waited thus, unmoved, during so many centuries, through the crises of so many things, that it could only be imagined to await one last crisis—the final overthrow.

It was a spot which returned upon the memory of those who loved it with an aspect of peculiar and kindly congruity. Smiling champaigns of flowers and fruit hardly do this, for they are permanently harmonious only with an existence of better reputation as to its issues than the present. Twilight combined with the scenery of Egdon Heath to evolve a thing majestic without severity, impressive without showiness, emphatic in its admonitions, grand in its simplicity. The qualifications which frequently invest the façade of a prison with far more dignity than is found in the façade of a palace double its size lent to this heath a sublimity in which spots renowned for beauty of the accepted kind are utterly wanting. Fair prospects wed happily with fair times; but alas, if times be not fair! Men have oftener suffered from the mockery of a place too smiling for their reason than from the oppression of surroundings oversadly tinged. Haggard Egdon appealed to a subtler and scarcer instinct, to a more recently learnt emotion, than that which responds to the sort of beauty called charming and fair.

Indeed, it is a question if the exclusive reign of this orthodox beauty is not approaching its last quarter. The new Vale of Tempe may be a gaunt waste in Thule: human souls may find themselves in closer and closer harmony with external things wearing a sombreness distasteful to our race when it was young. The time seems near, if it has not actually arrived, when the chastened sublimity of a moor, a sea, or a mountain will be all of nature that is absolutely in keeping with the moods of the more thinking among mankind. And ultimately, to the commonest tourist, spots like Iceland may become what the vineyards and myrtle-gardens of South Europe are to him now; and Heidelberg and Baden be passed unheeded as he hastens from the Alps to the sand-dunes of Scheveningen.

The most thorough-going ascetic could feel that he had a natural right to wander on Egdon: he was keeping within the line of legitimate indulgence when he laid himself open to influences such as these. Colours and beauties so far subdued were, at least, the birthright of all. Only in summer days of highest feather did its mood touch the level of gaiety. Intensity was more usually reached by way of the solemn than by way of the brilliant, and such a sort of intensity was often arrived at during winter darkness, tempests, and mists. Then Egdon was aroused to reciprocity; for the storm was its lover, and the wind its friend. Then it became the home of strange phantoms; and it was found to be the hitherto unrecognized original of those wild regions of obscurity which are vaguely felt to be compassing us about in midnight dreams of flight and disaster, and are never thought of after the dream till revived by scenes like this.

It was at present a place perfectly accordant with man's nature—neither ghastly, hateful, nor ugly: neither commonplace, unmeaning, nor tame; but, like man, slighted and enduring; and withal singularly colossal and mysterious in its swarthy monotony. As with some persons who have long lived apart, solitude seemed to look out of its countenance. It had a lonely face, suggesting tragical possibilities.

This obscure, obsolete, superseded country figures in Domesday. Its condition is recorded therein as that of heathy, furzy, briary wilderness—'Bruaria.' Then follows the length and breadth in leagues; and, though some uncertainty exists as to the exact extent of this ancient lineal measure, it appears from the figures that the area of Egdon down to the present day has but little diminished. 'Turbaria Bruaria'—the right of cutting heath-turf—occurs in charters relating to the district. 'Overgrown with heth and mosse,' says Leland of the same dark sweep of country.

Here at least were intelligible facts regarding landscape—far-reaching proofs productive of genuine satisfaction. The untameable, Ishmaelitish thing that Egdon now was it always had been. Civilization was its enemy; and ever since the beginning of vegetation its soil had worn the same antique brown dress, the natural and invariable garment of the particular formation. In its venerable one coat lay a certain vein of satire on human vanity in clothes. A person on a heath in raiment of modern cut and colours has more or less an anomalous look. We seem to want the oldest and simplest human clothing where the clothing of the earth is so primitive.

To recline on a stump of thorn in the central valley of Egdon, between afternoon and night, as now, where the eye could reach nothing of the world outside the summits and shoulders of heathland which filled the whole circumference of its glance, and to know that everything around and underneath had been from prehistoric times as unaltered as the stars overhead, gave ballast to the mind adrift on change, and harassed by the irrepressible New. The great inviolate place had an ancient permanence which the sea cannot claim. Who can say of a particular sea that it is old? Distilled by the sun, kneaded by the moon, it is renewed in a year, in a day, or in an hour. The sea changed, the fields changed, the rivers, the villages, and the people changed, yet Egdon remained. Those surfaces were neither so steep as to be destructible by weather, nor so flat as to be the victims of floods and deposits. With the exception of an aged highway, and a still more aged barrow . . . themselves almost crystallized to natural products by long continuance—even the trifling irregularities were not caused by pickaxe, plough, or spade, but remained as the very finger-touches of the last geological change.

The above-mentioned highway traversed the lower levels of the heath, from one horizon to another. In many portions of its course it overlaid an old vicinal way, which branched from the great Western road of the Romans, the Via Iceniana, or Ikenild Street, hard by. On the evening under consideration it would have been noticed that, though the gloom had increased sufficiently to confuse the minor features of the heath, the white surface of the road remained almost as clear as ever.

TEMPEST

CHARLES DICKENS

Nature often seems to sympathize with human moods. Poets and novelists have often used this phenomenon to heighten the emotional effect of their work, as Charles Dickens does in a chapter of his autobiographical novel, DAVID COPPERFIELD *(1850).*

The following episode occurs at a point in the story when the hero is in the throes of anxiety. His inner disquiet combines with the fury of the storm he encounters to create a tension which is truly excruciating.

David's childhood friend Emily has just returned to England and the welcoming arms of her uncle, Mr. Peggotty, after having run off to Europe with his old school friend and protector, Steerforth, who has now abandoned her. Emily and her uncle are due shortly to leave for Australia to take up a new life. The hero decides to set out from London to Yarmouth in order to deliver a message from Emily to Ham, her broken-hearted faithful lover. Little does he realize that at his destination, he will take his last farewell not only of Ham but of his old school chum who has caused so much tragedy. We take up the story as David is on the coach leaving London.

"Don't you think that," I asked the coachman, in the first stage out of London, "a very remarkable sky? I don't remember to have seen one like it."

"Nor I—not equal to it," he replied. "That's wind, sir. There'll be mischief done at sea, I expect, before long."

It was a murky confusion—here and there blotted with a colour like the colour of the smoke from damp fuel—of flying clouds tossed up into most remarkable heaps, suggesting greater heights in the clouds than there were depths below them to the bottom of the deepest hollows in the earth, through which the wild moon seemed to plunge headlong, as if, in a dread disturbance of the laws of nature, she had lost her way and were frightened. There had been a wind all day; and it was rising then, with an extraordinary great sound. In another hour it had much increased, and the sky was more overcast, and blew hard.

But as the night advanced, the clouds closing in and densely over-spreading the whole sky, then very dark, it came on to blow, harder and harder. It still increased, until our horses could scarcely face the wind. Many times, in the dark part of the night (it was then late in September, when the nights were not short), the leaders turned about, or came to a dead stop; and we were often in serious apprehension that the coach would be blown over. Sweeping gusts of rain came up before this storm, like showers of steel; and, at those times, when there was any shelter of trees or lee walls to be got, we were fain to stop, in a sheer impossibility of continuing the struggle.

When the day broke, it blew harder and harder. I had been in Yarmouth when the seamen said it blew great guns, but I had never known the like of this, or anything approaching to it. We came to Ipswich—very late, having had to fight every inch of ground since we were ten miles out of London; and found a cluster of people in the market-place, who had risen from their beds in the night, fearful of falling chimneys. Some of these, congregating about the inn-yard while we changed horses, told us of great sheets of lead having been ripped off a high church-tower, and flung into a bye-street, which they then blocked up. Others had to tell of country people, coming in from neighbouring villages, who had seen great trees lying torn out of the earth, and whole ricks scattered about the roads and fields. Still there was no abatement in the storm, but it blew harder.

As we struggled on, nearer and nearer to the sea, from which this mighty wind was blowing dead on shore, its force became more and more terrific. Long before we saw the sea, its spray was on our lips, and showered salt rain upon us. The water was out, over miles and miles of the flat country adjacent to Yarmouth; and every sheet and puddle lashed its banks, and had its stress of little breakers setting heavily towards us. When we came within sight of the sea, the waves on the horizon, caught at intervals above the rolling abyss, were like glimpses of another shore with towers and buildings. When at last we got into the town, the people came out to their doors, all aslant, and with streaming hair, making a wonder of the mail that had come through such a night.

I put up at the old inn, and went down to look at the sea; staggering along the street, which was strewn with sand and seaweed, and with flying blotches of sea-foam; afraid of falling slates and tiles; and holding by people I met, at angry corners. Coming near the beach, I saw, not only the boatmen, but half the people of the town, lurking behind buildings; some, now and then braving the fury of the storm to look away to sea, and blown sheer out of their course in trying to get zigzag back.

Joining these groups, I found bewailing women whose husbands were away in herring or oyster boats, which there was too much reason to think might have foundered before they could run in anywhere for safety. Grizzled old sailors were among the people, shaking their heads, as they looked from water to sky, and muttering to one another; ship-owners, excited and uneasy; children, huddling together, and peering into older faces; even stout mariners, disturbed and anxious, levelling their glasses at the sea from behind places of shelter, as if they were surveying an enemy.

The tremendous sea itself, when I could find sufficient pause to look at it, in the agitation of the blinding wind, the flying stones and sand, and the awful noise, confounded me. As the high watery walls came rolling in, and, at their highest, tumbled into surf, they looked as if the least would engulf the town. As the receding wave swept back with a horse roar, it seemed to scoop out deep caves in the beach, as if its purpose were to undermine the earth. When some white-headed billows thundered on, and dashed themselves to pieces before they reached the land, every fragment of the late whole seemed possessed by the full might of its wrath, rushing to be gathered to the composition of another monster. Undulating hills were changed to valleys, undulating valleys (with a solitary storm-bird sometimes skimming through them) were lifted up to hills; masses of water shivered and shook the beach with a booming sound; every shape tumultuously rolled on, as soon as made, to change its shape and place, and beat another shape and place away; the ideal shore on the horizon, with its towers and buildings, rose and fell; the clouds fell fast and thick; I seemed to see a rending and upheaving of all nature.

Not finding Ham among the people whom this memorable wind—for it is still remembered down there as the greatest ever known to blow upon that coast—had brought together, I made my way to his house. It was shut; and as no one answered to my knocking, I went, by back ways and bye-lanes, to the yard where he worked. I learned, there, that he had gone to Lowestoft, to meet some sudden exigency of ship-repairing in which his skill was required; but that he would be back to-morrow morning, in good time.

I went back to the inn; and when I had washed and dressed, and tried to sleep, but in vain, it was five o'clock in the afternoon. I had not sat five minutes by the coffee-room fire, when the waiter coming to stir it, as an excuse for talking, told me that two colliers had gone down, with all hands, a few miles away; and that some other ships had been seen labouring hard in the Roads, and trying, in great distress, to keep off shore. Mercy on them, and on all poor sailors, said he, if we had another night like the last!

I was very much depressed in spirits; very solitary; and felt an uneasiness in Ham's not being there, disproportionate to the occasion. I was seriously affected, without knowing how much, by late events; and my long exposure to the fierce wind had confused me. There was that jumble in my thoughts and recollections that I had lost the clear arrangement of time and distance. Thus, if I had gone out into the town, I should not have been surprised, I think, to encounter some one who I knew must be then in London. So to speak, there was in these respects a curious inattention in my mind. Yet it was busy, too, with all the remembrances the place naturally awakened; and they were particularly distinct and vivid.

In this state, the waiter's dismal intelligence about the ships immediately connected itself, without any effort of my volition, with my uneasiness about Ham. I was persuaded that I had an apprehension of his returning from Lowestoft by sea, and being lost. This grew so strong with me, that I resolved to go back to the yard before I took my dinner, and ask the boat-builder if he thought his attempting to return by sea at all likely? If he gave me the least reason to think so I would go over to Lowestoft and prevent it by bringing him with me.

I hastily ordered my dinner, and went back to the yard. I was none too soon; for the boat-builder, with a lantern in his hand, was locking the yard-gate. He quite laughed when I asked him the question, and said there was no fear; no man in his senses, or out of them, would put off in such a gale of wind, least of all Ham Peggotty, who had been born to seafaring.

So sensible of this, beforehand, that I had really felt ashamed of doing what I was nevertheless impelled to do, I went back to the inn. If such a wind could rise, I think it was rising. The howl and roar, the rattling of the doors and windows, the rumbling in the chimneys, the apparent rocking of the very house that sheltered me, and the prodigious tumult of the sea, were more fearful than in the morning. But there was now a great darkness besides; and that invested the storm with new terrors, real and fanciful.

I could not eat, I could not sit still, I could not continue stedfast to anything. Something within me, faintly answering to the storm without, tossed up the depths of my memory and made a tumult in them. Yet, in all the hurry of my thoughts, wild running with the thundering sea—the storm and my uneasiness regarding Ham were always in the foreground.

My dinner went away almost untasted, and I tried to refresh myself with a glass or two of wine. In vain. I fell into a dull slumber before the fire, without losing my consciousness, either of the uproar out of doors, or of the place in which I was. Both became over-shadowed by a new and indefinable horror; and when I awoke—or rather when I shook off the lethargy that bound me in my chair—my whole frame thrilled with objectless and unintelligible fear.

I walked to and fro, tried to read an old gazetteer, listened to the awful noises: looked at faces, scenes and figures in the fire. At length, the steady ticking of the undisturbed clock on the wall tormented me to that degree that I resolved to go to bed.

It was reassuring, on such a night, to be told that some of the inn-servants had agreed together to sit up until morning. I went to bed, exceedingly weary and heavy; but, on my lying down, all such sensations vanished, as if by magic, and I was broad awake, with every sense refined.

For hours I lay there, listening to the wind and water; imagining, now, that I heard shrieks out at sea; now, that I distinctly heard the firing of signal guns; and now, the fall of houses in the town. I got up several times, and looked out; but could see nothing, except the reflection in the window-panes of the faint candle I had left burning, and of my own haggard face looking in at me from the black void.

At length, my restlessness attained to such a pitch, that I hurried on my clothes, and went down-stairs. In the large kitchen, where I dimly saw bacon and ropes of onions hanging from the beams, the watchers were clustered together, in various attitudes, about a table, purposely moved away from the great chimney, and brought near the door. A pretty girl, who had her ears stopped with her apron, and her eyes upon the door, screamed when I appeared, supposing me to be a spirit; but the others had more presence of mind, and were glad of an addition to their company. One man, referring to the topic they had been discussing, asked me whether I thought the souls of the collier-crews who had gone down, were out in the storm?

I remained there, I dare say, two hours. Once, I opened the yard-gate, and looked into the empty street. The sand, the seaweed, and the flakes of foam, were driving by; and I was obliged to call for assistance before I could shut the gate again, and make it fast against the wind.

There was a dark gloom in my solitary chamber, when I at length returned to it; but I was tired now, and, getting into bed again, fell–off a tower and down a precipice–into the depths of sleep. I have an impression that for a long time, though I dreamed of being elsewhere and in a variety of scenes, it was always blowing in my dream. At length, I lost that feeble hold upon reality, and was engaged with two dear friends, but who they were I don't know, at the siege of some town in a roar of cannonading.

The thunder of the cannon was so loud and incessant, that I could not hear something I much desired to hear, until I made a great exertion and awoke. It was broad day–eight or nine o'clock; the storm raging, in lieu of the batteries; and some one knocking and calling at my door.

"What is the matter?" I cried.

"A wreck! Close by!"

I sprung out of bed, and asked, what wreck?

"A schooner, from Spain or Portugal, laden with fruit and wine. Make haste, sir, if you want to see her! It's thought, down on the beach, she'll go to pieces every moment."

The excited voice went clamouring along the staircase; and I wrapped myself in my clothes as quickly as I could, and ran into the street.

Numbers of people were there before me, all running in one

direction to the beach. I ran the same way, outstripping a good many, and soon came facing the wild sea.

The wind might by this time have lulled a little, though not more sensibly than if the cannonading I had dreamed of had been diminished by the silencing of half-a-dozen guns out of hundreds. But the sea, having upon it the additional agitation of the whole night, was infinitely more terrific than when I had seen it last. Every appearance it had then presented, bore the expression of being *swelled;* and the height to which the breakers rose, and, looking over one another, bore one another down, and rolled in, in interminable hosts, was most appalling.

In the difficulty of hearing anything but wind and waves, and in the crowd, and the unspeakable confusion, and my first breathless efforts to stand against the weather, I was so confused that I looked out to sea for the wreck, and saw nothing but the foaming heads of the great waves. A half-dressed boatman, standing next me, pointed with his bare arm (a tattoo'd arrow on it, pointing in the same direction) to the left. Then, O great Heaven, I saw it, close in upon us!

One mast was broken short off, six or eight feet from the deck, and lay over the side, entangled in a maze of sail and rigging; and all that ruin, as the ship rolled and beat—which she did without a moment's pause, and with a violence quite inconceivable—beat the side as if it would stave it in. Some efforts were even then being made, to cut this portion of the wreck away; for as the ship, which was broadside on, turned towards us in her rolling, I plainly descried her people at work with axes, especially one active figure with long curling hair, conspicuous among the rest. But a great cry, which was audible even above the wind and water, rose from the shore at this moment; the sea, sweeping over the rolling wreck, made a clean breach, and carried men, spars, casts, planks, bulwarks, heaps of such toys, into the boiling surge.

The second mast was yet standing, with the rags of a rent sail, and a wild confusion of broken cordage flapping to and fro. The ship had struck once, the same boatman hoarsely said in my ear, and then lifted in and struck again. I understood him to add that she was parting amidships, and I could readily suppose so, for the rolling and beating were too tremendous for any human work to suffer long. As he spoke, there was another great cry of pity from the beach; four men arose with the wreck out of the deep, clinging to the rigging of the remaining mast; uppermost, the active figure with the curling hair.

There was a bell on board; and as the ship rolled and dashed, like a desperate creature driven mad, now showing us the whole sweep of her deck, as she turned on her beam-ends towards the shore, now nothing but her keel, as she sprung wildly over and turned towards the sea, the bell rang; and its sound, the knell of those unhappy men, was borne towards us on the wind. Again we lost her, and again she rose. Two men were gone. The agony on shore increased. Men groaned, and clasped their hands; women shrieked, and turned away their faces. Some ran wildly up and down along the beach crying for help where no help could be. I found myself one of these, frantically imploring a knot of sailors whom I knew, not to let those two lost creatures perish before our eyes.

They were making out to me, in an agitated way–I don't know how, for the little I could hear I was scarcely composed enough to understand–that the lifeboat had been bravely manned an hour ago, and could do nothing; and that as no man would be so desperate as to attempt to wade off with a rope, and establish a communication with the shore, there was nothing left to try; when I noticed that some new sensation moved the people on the beach, and saw them part, and Ham come breaking through them to the front.

I ran to him–as well as I know–to repeat my appeal for help. But, distracted though I was by a sight so new to me and terrible, the determination in his face, and his look out to sea–exactly the same look as I remembered in connexion with the morning after Emily's flight–awoke me to a knowledge of his danger. I held him back with both arms; and implored the men with whom I had been speaking, not to listen to him, not to do murder, not to let him stir from off that sand!

Another cry arose on shore; and looking to the wreck, we saw the cruel sail, with blow on blow, beat off the lower of the two men, and fly up in triumph round the active figure left alone upon the mast.

Against such a sight, and against such determination as that of the calmly desperate man who was already accustomed to lead half the people present, I might as hopefully have entreated the wind. "Mas'r Davy," he said, cheerily grasping me by both hands, "if my time is come, 'tis come. If 'tain't, I'll bide it. Lord above bless you, and bless all! Mates, make me ready! I'm a-going off!"

I was swept away, but not unkindly, to some distance, where the people around made me stay, urging, as I confusedly perceived, that he was bent on going, with help or without, and that I should endanger the precautions for his safety by troubling those with whom they rested. I don't know what I answered, or what they rejoined; but I saw hurry on the beach, and men running with ropes from a capstan that was there, and penetrating into a circle of figures that hid him from me. Then I saw him standing alone, in a seaman's frock and trowsers: a rope in his hand, or slung to his wrist; another round his body; and several of the best men holding, at a little distance, to the latter, which he laid out himself, slack upon the shore, at his feet.

The wreck, even to my unpractised eye, was breaking up. I saw that she was parting in the middle, and that the life of the solitary man upon the mast hung by a thread. Still, he clung to it. He had a singular red cap on–not like a sailor's cap, but of a finer colour; and as the few yielding planks between him and destruction rolled and bulged, and his anticipative death-knell rung, he was seen by all of us to wave it. I saw him do it now, and thought I was going distracted, when his action brought an old remembrance to my mind of a once dear friend.

Ham watched the sea, standing alone, with the silence of suspended breath behind him, and the storm before, until there was a great retiring wave, when, with a backward glance at those who held the rope which was made fast round his body, he dashed in after it, and in a moment was buffeting with the water; rising with the hills, falling with the valleys, lost beneath the foam; then drawn again to land. They hauled in hastily.

He was hurt. I saw blood on his face, from where I stood; but he took no thought of that. He seemed hurriedly to give them some directions for leaving him more free–or so I judged from the motion of his arm–and was gone as before.

And now he made for the wreck, rising with the hills, falling with the valleys, lost beneath the rugged foam, borne in towards the shore, borne on towards the ship, striving hard and valiantly. The distance was nothing, but the power of the sea and wind made the strife deadly. At length he neared the wreck. He was so near, that with one more of his vigorous strokes he would be clinging to it—when a high, green, vast hill-side of water, moving on shoreward, from beyond the ship, he seemed to leap into it with a mighty bound, and the ship was gone!

Some eddying fragments I saw in the sea, as if a mere cask had been broken, in running to the spot where they were hauling in. Consternation was in every face. They drew him to my very feet —insensible—dead. He was carried to the nearest house; and, no one preventing me now, I remained near him, busy, while every means of restoration were tried; but he had been beaten to death by the great wave, and his generous heart was stilled for ever.

As I sat beside the bed, when hope was abandoned and all was done, a fisherman, who had known me when Emily and I were children, and ever since, whispered my name at the door.

"Sir," said he, with tears starting to his weather-beaten face, which, with his trembling lips, was ashy pale, "will you come over yonder?"

The old remembrance that had been recalled to me, was in his look. I asked him, terror-stricken, leaning on the arm he held out to support me:

"Has a body come ashore?"

He said, "Yes."

"Do I know it?" I asked then.

He answered nothing.

But he led me to the shore. And on that part of it where she and I had looked for shells, two children—on that part of it where some lighter fragments of the old boat, blown down last night, had been scattered by the wind—among the ruins of the home he had wronged—I saw him lying with his head upon his arm, as I had often seen him lie at school.

EARTHQUAKE STORMS

JOHN MUIR

—a selection from The Yosemite *by John Muir, Century Co., 1912.*
John Muir was an amateur naturalist who spent much time in the California mountains. It was largely as a result of a series of articles he wrote for Century Magazine *that, in 1890, Yosemite and Sequoia national parks were established. One of his most stirring pieces of descriptive writing concerns a violent earthquake in the Yosemite area. This particular cataclysm not only impressed the author with its awesome beauty, but also satisfied his scientific curiosity in regard to the formation of certain mysterious avalanche taluses.*

At half-past two o'clock of a moonlit morning in March, I was awakened by a tremendous earthquake, and though I had never before enjoyed a storm of this sort, the strange thrilling motion could not be mistaken, and I ran out of my cabin, both glad and frightened, shouting, "A noble earthquake! A noble earthquake!" feeling sure I was going to learn something. The shocks were so violent and varied, and succeeded one another so closely, that I had to balance myself carefully in walking as if on the deck of a ship among waves, and it seemed impossible that the high cliffs of the Valley could escape being shattered. In particular, I feared that the sheer-fronted Sentinel Rock, towering above my cabin, would be shaken down, and I took shelter back of a large yellow pine, hoping that it might protect me from at least the smaller out-bounding boulders. For a minute or two the shocks became more and more violent—flashing horizontal thrusts mixed with a few twists and battering, explosive, upheaving jolts,—as if Nature were wrecking her Yosemite temple, and getting ready to build a still better one.

I was now convinced before a single boulder had fallen that earthquakes were the talus-makers and positive proof soon came. It was a calm moonlight night, and no sound was heard for the first minute or so, save low, muffled, underground, bubbling rumblings, and the whispering and rustling of the agitated trees, as if Nature were holding her breath. Then, suddenly, out of the strange silence and strange motion there came a tremendous roar. The Eagle Rock on the south wall, about a half a mile up the Valley, gave way and I saw it falling in thousands of the great boulders I had so long been studying, pouring to the Valley floor in a free curve luminous from friction, making a terribly sublime spectacle—an arc of glowing, passionate fire, fifteen hundred feet span, as true in form and as serene in beauty as a rainbow in the midst of the stupendous, roaring rock-storm. The sound was so tremendously deep and broad and earnest, the whole earth like a living creature seemed to have at last found a voice and to be calling to her sister planets. In trying to tell something of the size of this awful sound it seems to me that if all the thunder of all the storms I had ever heard were condensed into one roar it would not equal this rock-roar at the birth of a mountain talus. Think, then, of the roar that arose to heaven at the simultaneous birth of all the thousands of ancient canyon-taluses throughout the length and breadth of the range!

The first severe shocks were soon over, and eager to examine the new-born talus I ran up the Valley in the moonlight and climbed upon it before the huge blocks, after their fiery flight, had come to complete rest. They were slowly settling into their places, chafing, grating against one another, groaning, and whispering; but no motion was visible except in a stream of small fragments pattering down the face of the cliff. A cloud of dust particles, lighted by the moon, floated out across the whole breadth of the Valley, forming a ceiling that lasted until after sunrise, and the air was filled with the odor of crushed Douglas spruces from a grove that had been mowed down and mashed like weeds.

After the ground began to calm I ran across the meadow to the river to see in what direction it was flowing and was glad to find that *down* the Valley was still down. Its waters were muddy from portions of its banks having given way, but it was flowing around its curves and over its ripples and shallows with ordinary tones and gestures. The mud would soon be cleared away and the raw slips on the banks would be the only visible record of the shaking it suffered.

The Upper Yosemite Fall, glowing white in the moonlight, seemed to know nothing of the earthquake, manifesting no change in form or voice, as far as I could see or hear.

After a second startling shock, about half-past three o'clock, the ground continued to tremble gently, and smooth, hollow rumbling sounds, not always distinguishable from the rounded, bumping, explosive tones of the falls, came from deep in the mountains in a northern direction.

The few Indians fled from their huts to the middle of the Valley, fearing that angry spirits were trying to kill them; and as I afterward learned, most of the Yosemite tribe, who were spending the winter at their village on Bull Creek forty miles away, were so terrified that they ran into the river and washed themselves,—getting themselves clean enough to say their prayers, I suppose, or to die. I asked Dick, one of the Indians with whom I was acquainted, "What made the ground shake and jump so much?" He only shook his head and said, "No good. No good," and looked appealingly to me to give him hope that his life was to be spared.

In the morning I found the few white settlers assembled in front of the old Hutchings Hotel comparing notes and meditating flight to the lowlands, seemingly as sorely frightened as the Indians. Shortly after sunrise a low, blunt, muffled rumbling, like distant thunder, was followed by another series of shocks, which, though not nearly so severe as the first, made the cliffs and domes tremble like jelly, and the big pines and oaks thrill and swish and wave their branches with startling effect. Then the talkers were suddenly hushed, and the solemnity on their faces was sublime. One in particular of these winter neighbors, a somewhat speculative thinker with whom I had often conversed, was a firm believer in the cataclysmic origin of the Valley; and I now jokingly remarked that his wild tumble-down-and-engulfment hypothesis might soon be proved, since these underground rumblings and shakings might be the forerunners of another Yosemite-making cataclysm, which would perhaps double the depth of the Valley by swallowing the floor, leaving the ends of the roads and trails dangling three or four thousand feet in the air. Just then came the third series of shocks, and it was fine to see how awfully silent and solemn he became. His belief in the existence of a mysterious abyss, into which the suspended floor of the Valley and all the domes and battlements of the walls might at any moment go roaring down, mightily troubled him. To diminish his fears and laugh him into something like reasonable faith, I said, "Come, cheer up; smile a little and clap your hands, now that kind Mother Earth is trotting us on her knee to amuse us and make us good." But the well-meant joke seemed irreverent and utterly failed, as if only prayerful terror could rightly belong to the wild beauty-making business. Even after all the heavier shocks were over I could do nothing to reassure him. On the contrary, he handed me the keys to his little store to keep, saying that with a companion of like mind he was going to the lowlands to stay until the fate of poor, trembling Yosemite was settled. In vain I rallied them on their fears, calling attention to the strength of the granite walls of our Valley home, the very best and solidist masonry in the world, and less likely to collapse and sink than the sedimentary lowlands to which they were looking for safety; and saying that in any case they sometime would have to die, and so grand a burial was not to be slighted. But they were too seriously panic-stricken to get comfort from anything I could say.

During the third severe shock the trees were so violently shaken that the birds flew out with frightened cries. In particular, I noticed two robins flying in terror from a leafless oak, the branches of which swished and quivered as if struck by a heavy battering-ram. Exceedingly interesting were the flashing and quivering of the elastic needles of the pines in the sunlight and the waving up and down of the branches while the trunks stood rigid. There was no swaying, waving or swirling as in windstorms, but quick, quivering jerks, and at times the heavy tasseled branches moved as if they had all been pressed down against the trunk and suddenly let go, to spring up and vibrate until they came to rest again. Only the owls seemed to be undisturbed. Before the rumbling echoes had died away a hollow-voiced owl began to hoot in philosophical tranquillity from near the edge of the new talus as if nothing extraordinary had occurred, although, perhaps, he was curious to know what all the noise was about. His "hoot-too-hoot-too-whoo" might have meant, "what's a' the steer, kimmer?"

It was long before the Valley found perfect rest. The rocks trembled more or less every day for over two months, and I kept a bucket of water on my table to learn what I could of the movements. The blunt thunder in the depths of the mountains was usually followed by sudden jarring horizontal thrusts from the northward, often succeeded by twisting, upjolting movements. More than a month after the first great shock, when I was standing on a fallen tree up the Valley near Lamon's winter cabin, I heard a distinct bubbling thunder from the direction of Tenaya Canyon. Carlo, a large intelligent St. Bernard dog standing beside me, seemed greatly astonished, and looked intently in that direction with mouth open and uttered a low *Wouf!* as if saying, "What's that?" He must have known that it was not thunder, though like it. The air was perfectly still, not the faintest breath of wind perceptible, and a fine, mellow, sunny hush pervaded everything, in the midst of which came that subterranean thunder. Then, while we gazed and listened, came the corresponding shocks, distinct as if some mighty hand had shaken the ground. After the sharp horizontal jars died away, they were followed by a gentle rocking and undulating of the ground so distinct that Carlo looked at the log on which he was standing to see who was shaking it. It was the season of flooded meadows and the pools about me, calm as sheets of glass, were suddenly thrown into low ruffling waves.

Judging by its effects, this Yosemite, or Inyo earthquake, as it is sometimes called, was gentle as compared with the one that gave rise to the grand talus system of the range and did so much for the canyon scenery. Nature, usually so deliberate in her operations, then created, as we have seen, a new set of features, simply by giving the mountains a shake–changing not only the high peaks and cliffs, but the streams. As soon as these rock avalanches fell, the streams began to sing new songs; for in many places thousands of boulders were hurled into their channels, roughening and half-damming them, compelling the waters to surge and roar in rapids where before they glided smoothly. Some of the streams were completely dammed; driftwood, leaves, etc., gradually filling the interstices between the boulders, thus giving rise to lakes and level reaches; and these again, after being gradually filled in, were changed to meadows, through which the streams are now silently meandering; while at the same time some of the taluses took the places of old meadows and groves. Thus rough places were made smooth, and smooth places rough. But, on the whole, by what at first sight seemed pure confounded confusion and ruin, the landscapes were enriched; for gradually every talus was covered with groves and gardens, and made a finely proportioned and ornamental base for the cliffs. In this work of beauty, every boulder is prepared and measured and put in its place more thoughtfully than are the stones of temples. If for a moment you are inclined to regard these taluses as mere draggled, chaotic dumps, climb to the top of one of them, and run down without any haggling, puttering hesitation, boldly jumping from boulder to boulder with even speed. You will then find your feet playing a tune, and quickly discover the music and poetry of these magnificent rock piles—a fine lesson; and all Nature's wildness tells the same story—the shocks and outbursts of earthquakes, volcanoes, geysers, roaring, thundering waves and floods, the silent uprush of sap in plants, storms of every sort—each and all are the orderly beauty-making love-beats of Nature's heart.

THE GRAND CAÑON of the COLORADO

JOHN WESLEY POWELL

—a selection from Exploration of the Colorado River of the West and Its Tributaries, *a report to the Smithsonian Institution by John Wesley Powell in 1875.*

John Wesley Powell was a bearded, one-armed Civil War veteran who led a group of adventurers in 1869 through the then unknown rapids of the Green and Colorado rivers. They were the first to explore the many cañons in Utah and Arizona, and the climax of their trip was the perilous ride through the Grand Cañon, part of which is described here.

The little band of brave men started out from Green River, Wyoming in March, 1869. Our account begins shortly after their reaching the Grand Cañon in mid-August.

We can see but a little way into the granite gorge, but it looks threatening.

After breakfast we enter on the waves. At the very introduction, it inspires awe. The cañon is narrower than we have ever before seen it; the water is swifter; there are but few broken rocks in the channel; but the walls are set, on either side, with pinnacles and crags; and sharp, angular buttresses, bristling with wind and wave polished spires, extend far out into the river.

Ledges of rocks jut into the stream, their tops sometimes just below the surface, sometimes rising few or many feet above; and island ledges, and island pinnacles, and island towers break the swift course of the stream into chutes, and eddies, and whirlpools. We soon reach a place where a creek comes in from the left, and just below, the channel is choked with boulders, which have washed down this lateral cañon and formed a dam, over which there is a fall of thirty or forty feet; but on the boulders we can get foothold, and we make a portage.

Three more such dams are found. Over one we make a portage; at the other two we find chutes, through which we can run.

As we proceed, the granite rises higher, until nearly a thousand feet of the lower part of the walls are composed of this rock.

About eleven o'clock we hear a great roar ahead, and approach it very cautiously. The sound grows louder and louder as we run, and at last we find ourselves above a long, broken fall, with ledges and pinnacles of rock obstructing the river. There is a descent of, perhaps, seventy-five or eighty feet in a third of a mile, and the rushing waters break into great waves on the rocks, and lash themselves into a mad, white foam. We can land just above, but there is no foothold on either side by which we can make a portage. It is nearly a thousand feet to the top of the granite, so it will be impossible to carry our boats around, though we can climb to the summit up a side gulch, and passing along a mile or two, can descend to the river. This we find on examination; but such a portage would be impracticable for us, and we must run the rapid, or abandon the river. There is no hesitation. We step into our boats, push off and away we go, first on smooth but swift water, then we strike a glassy wave, and ride to its top, down again into the trough, up again on a higher wave, and down and up on waves higher and still higher, until we strike one just as it curls back, and a breaker rolls over our little boat. Still, on we speed, shooting past projecting rocks, till the little boat is caught in a whirlpool, and spun around several times. At last we pull out again into the stream, and now the other boats have passed us. The open compartment of the "Emma Dean" is filled with water, and every breaker rolls over us. Hurled back from a rock, now on this side, now on that, we are carried into an eddy, in which we struggle for a few minutes, and are then out again, the breakers still rolling over us. Our boat is unmanageable, but she cannot sink, and we drift down another hundred yards, through breakers; how, we scarcely know. We find the other boats have turned into an eddy at the foot of the fall, and are waiting to catch us as we come, for the men have seen that our boat is swamped. They push out as we come near, and pull us in against the wall. We bail our boat, and on we go again.

The walls, now, are more than a mile in height—a vertical

distance difficult to appreciate. Stand on the south steps of the Treasury building, in Washington, and look down Pennsylvania Avenue to the Capitol Park, and measure this distance overhead, and imagine cliffs to extend to that altitude, and you will understand what I mean; or stand at Canal street, in New York, and look up Broadway to Grace Church, and you have about the distance; or, stand at Lake street bridge, in Chicago, and look down to the Central Depot, and you have it again.

A thousand feet of this is up through granite crags, then steep slopes and perpendicular cliffs rise, one above another, to the summit. The gorge is black and narrow below, red and gray and flaring above, with crags and angular projections on the walls, which, cut in many places by side cañons, seem to be a vast wilderness of rocks. Down in these grand, gloomy depths we glide, ever listening, for the mad waters keep up their roar; ever watching, ever peering ahead, for the narrow cañon is winding, and the river is closed in so that we can see but a few hundred yards, and what there may be below we know not; but we listen for falls, and watch for rocks, or stop now and then, in the bay of a recess, to admire the gigantic scenery. And ever, as we go, there is some new pinnacle or tower, some crag or peak, some distant view of the upper plateau, some strange-shaped rock, or some deep, narrow side cañon. Then we come to another broken fall, which appears more difficult than the one we ran this morning.

A small creek comes in on the right, and the first fall of the water is over boulders, which have been carried down by this lateral stream. We land at its mouth, and stop for an hour or two to examine the fall. It seems possible to let down with lines, at least a part of the way, from point to point, along the right-hand wall. So we make a portage over the first rocks, and find footing on some boulders below. Then we let down one of the boats to the end of her line, when she reaches a corner of the projecting rock, to which one of the men clings, and steadies her, while I examine an eddy below. I think we can pass the other boats down by us, and catch them in the eddy. This is soon done and the men in the boats in the eddy pull us to their side. On the shore of this little eddy there is about two feet of gravel beach above the water. Standing on this beach, some of the men take the line of the little boat and let it drift down against another projecting angle. Here is a little shelf, on which a man from my boat climbs, and a shorter line is passed to him, and he fastens the boat to the side of the cliff. Then the second one is let down, bringing the line of the third. When the second boat is tied up, the two men standing on the beach above spring into the last boat, which is pulled up alongside of ours. Then we let down the boats, for twenty-five or thirty yards, by walking along the shelf, landing them again in the mouth of a side cañon. Just below this there is another pile of boulders, over which we make another portage. From the foot of these rocks we can climb to another shelf, forty or fifty feet above the water.

On this bench we camp for the night. We find a few sticks, which have lodged in the rocks. It is raining hard, and we have no shelter, but kindle a fire and have our supper. We sit on the rocks all night, wrapped in our ponchos, getting what sleep we can.

August 15.—This morning we find we can let down for three or four hundred yards, and it is managed in this way: We pass along the wall, by climbing from projecting point to point, sometimes near the water's edge, at other places fifty or sixty feet above, and hold the boat with a line, while two men remain aboard, and prevent her from being dashed against the rocks, and keep the line from getting caught on the wall. In two hours we have brought them all down, as far as it is possible, in this way. A few yards below, the river strikes with great violence against a projecting rock, and our boats are pulled up in a little bay above. We must now manage to pull out of this, and clear the point below. The little boat is held by the bow obliquely up the stream. We jump in, and pull out only a few strokes, and sweep clear of the dangerous rock. The other boats follow in the same manner, and the rapid is passed.

It is not easy to describe the labor of such navigation. We must prevent the waves from dashing the boats against the cliffs. Sometimes, where the river is swift, we must put a bight of rope about a rock, to prevent her being snatched from us by a wave; but where the plunge is too great, or the chute too swift, we must let her leap, and catch her below, or the undertow will drag her under the falling water, and she sinks. Where we wish to run her out a little way from shore, through a channel between rocks, we first throw in little sticks of driftwood, and watch their course, to see where we must steer, so that she will pass the channel in safety. And so we hold, and let go, and pull, and lift, and ward, among rocks, around rocks, and over rocks.

And now we go on through this solemn, mysterious way. The river is very deep, the cañon very narrow, and still obstructed, so that there is no steady flow of the stream; but the waters wheel, and roll, and boil, and we are scarcely able to determine where we can go. Now, the boat is carried to the right, perhaps close to the wall; again, she is shot into the stream, and perhaps is dragged over to the other side, where, caught in a whirlpool, she spins about. We can neither land nor run as we please. The boats are entirely unmanageable; no order in their running can be preserved; now one, now another, is ahead, each crew laboring for its own preservation. In such a place we come to another rapid. Two of the boats run it perforce. One succeeds in landing, but there is no foothold by which to make a portage, and she is pushed out again into the stream. The next minute a great reflex wave fills the open compartment; she is water-logged, and drifts unmanageable. Breaker after breaker rolls over her, and one capsizes her. The men are thrown out; but they cling to the boat, and she drifts down some distance, alongside of us, and we are able to catch her. She is soon bailed out, and the men are aboard once more; but the oars are lost, so a pair from the "Emma Dean" is spared. Then for two miles we find smooth water.

Clouds are playing in the cañon today. Sometimes they roll down in great masses, filling the gorge with gloom; sometimes they hang above, from wall to wall, and cover the cañon with a roof of impending storm; and we can peer long distances up and down this cañon corridor, with its cloud roof overhead, its walls of black granite, and its river bright with the sheen of broken waters. Then, a gust of wind sweeps down a side gulch, and, making a rift in the clouds, reveals the blue heavens, and a stream of sunlight pours in. Then, the clouds drift away into the distance, and hang around crags, and peaks, and pinnacles, and towers, and walls, and cover them with a mantle, that lifts from time to time, and sets them all in sharp relief. Then, baby clouds creep out of side cañons, glide around points, and creep back again, into more distant gorges. Then, clouds, set in strata, across the cañon, with intervening vista views, to cliffs and rocks beyond. The clouds are children of the heavens, and when they play among the rocks, they lift them to the region above.

It rains! Rapidly little rills are formed above, and these soon grow into brooks, and the brooks grow into creeks, and tumble over the walls in innumerable cascades, adding their wild music to the roar of the river. When the rain ceases, the rills, brooks, and creeks run dry. The waters that fall, during a rain, on these steep rocks, are gathered at once into the river; they could scarcely be poured in more suddenly, if some vast spout ran from the clouds to the stream itself. When a storm bursts over the cañon, a side gulch is dangerous, for a sudden flood may come, and the inpouring waters will raise the river, so as to hide the rocks before your eyes.

Early in the afternoon, we discover a stream, entering from the north, a clear, beautiful creek, coming down through a gorgeous red cañon. We land, and camp on a sand beach, above its mouth, under a great, overspreading tree, with willow-shaped leaves. . . .

August 17.—Our rations are still spoiling; the bacon is so badly injured that we are compelled to throw it away. By an accident, this morning, the saleratus is lost overboard. We have now only musty flour sufficient for ten days, a few dried apples, but plenty of coffee. We must make all haste possible. If we meet with difficulties, as we have done in the cañon above, we may be compelled to give up the expedition, and try to reach the Mormon settlements to the north. Our hopes are that the worst places are passed, but our barometers are all so much injured as to be useless, so we have lost our reckoning in altitude, and know not how much descent the river has yet to make.

The stream is still wild and rapid, and rolls through a narrow channel. We make but slow progress, often landing against a wall, and climbing around some point, where we can see the river below. Although very anxious to advance, we are determined to run with great caution, lest, by another accident, we lose all our supplies. How precious that little flour has become! We divide it among the boats, and carefully store it away, so that it can be lost only by the loss of the boat itself.

We make ten miles and a half, and camp among the rocks, on the right. We have had rain, from time to time, all day, and have been thoroughly drenched and chilled; but between showers the sun shines with great power, and the mercury in our thermometers stands at 115°, so that we have rapid changes from great extremes, which are very disagreeable. It is especially cold in the rain tonight. The little canvas we have is rotten and useless; the rubber ponchos, with which we started from Green River

City, have all been lost; more than half the party is without hats, and not one of us has an entire suit of clothes, and we have not a blanket apiece. So we gather driftwood, and build a fire; but after supper the rain, coming down in torrents, extinguishes it, and we sit up all night, on the rocks, shivering, and are more exhausted by the night's discomfort than by the day's toil.

August 18.—The day is employed in making portages, and we advance but two miles on our journey. Still it rains.

While the men are at work making portages, I climb up the granite to its summit, and go away back over the rust-colored sandstones and greenish-yellow shales, to the foot of the marble wall. I climb so high that the men and boats are lost in the black depths below, and the dashing river is a rippling brook; and still there is more cañon above than below. All about me are interesting geological records. The book is open, and I can read as I run. All about me are grand views, for the clouds are playing again in the gorges. But somehow I think of the nine day's rations, and the bad river, and the lesson of the rocks, and the glory of the scene is but half seen.

I push on to an angle, where I hope to get a view of the country beyond, to see, if possible, what the prospect may be of our soon running through this plateau, or at least, of meeting with some geological change that will let us out of the granite; but, arriving at the point, I can see below only a labyrinth of deep gorges.

August 19.—Rain again this morning. Still we are in our granite prison, and the time is occupied until noon in making a long, bad portage.

After dinner, in running a rapid, the pioneer boat is upset by a wave. We are some distance in advance of the larger boats, the river is rough and swift, and we are unable to land, but cling to the boat, and are carried down stream, over another rapid. The men in the boats above see our trouble, but they are caught in whirlpools, and are spinning about in eddies, and it seems a long time before they come to our relief. At last they do come; our boat is turned right side up, bailed out; the oars, which fortunately have floated along in company with us, are gathered up, and on we go, without even landing.

Soon after the accident the clouds break away, and we have sunshine again.

Soon we find a little beach, with just room enough to land.

Here we camp, but there is no wood. Across the river, and a little way above, we see some driftwood lodged in the rocks. So we bring two boat loads over, build a huge fire, and spread everything to dry. It is the first cheerful night we have had for a week; a warm, drying fire in the midst of the camp, and a few bright stars in our patch of heavens overhead.

THE LOST ONE

JOHN JAMES AUDUBON

The famous American ornithologist, John James Audubon, earned his livelihood by painting wildlife. In 1821 he left his family to go alone into the wilderness of the southeastern United States. Three years later he returned with over a thousand of his famous drawings, which were published in London, during the period 1827-1838, under the title THE BIRDS OF AMERICA. *In collaboration with William MacGillivray, who was responsible for its scientific information, Audubon wrote an accompanying text for this work entitled* ORNITHOLOGICAL BIOGRAPHY, *which was published in five volumes in Edinburgh from 1831 to 1839. The essay reprinted here is one of the many sketches of American frontier life which the renowned ornithologist wrote to enliven the pages of the* BIOGRAPHY.

A "live-oaker," employed on the St. John's River, in East Florida, left his cabin, situated on the banks of that stream, and with his axe on his shoulder proceeded towards the swamp in which he had several times before plied his trade of felling and squaring the giant trees that afford the most valuable timber for naval architecture and other purposes.

At the season which is the best for this kind of labour, heavy fogs not unfrequently cover the country, so as to render it difficult for one to see farther than thirty or forty yards in any direction. The woods, too, present so little variety, that every tree seems the mere counterpart of every other; and the grass, when it has not been burnt, is so tall that a man of ordinary stature cannot see over it, whence it is necessary for him to proceed with great caution, lest he should unwittingly deviate from the ill-defined trail which he follows. To increase the difficulty, several trails often meet, in which case, unless the explorer be perfectly acquainted with the neighbourhood, it would be well for him to lie down, and wait until the fog should disperse. Under such circumstances the best woodsmen are not unfrequently bewildered for a while; and I well remember that such an occurrence happened to myself, at a time when I had imprudently ventured to pursue a wounded quadruped, which led me some distance from the track.

The live-oaker had been jogging onwards for several hours, and became aware that he must have travelled considerably more than the distance between his cabin and the "hummock" which he desired to reach. To his alarm, at the moment when the fog dispersed, he saw the sun at its meridian height, and could not recognise a single object around him.

Young, healthy, and active, he imagined that he had walked with more than usual speed, and had passed the place to which he was bound. He accordingly turned his back upon the sun, and pursued a different route, guided by a small trail. Time passed, and the sun headed his course: he saw it gradually descend in the west; but all around him continued as if enveloped with mystery. The huge gray trees spread their giant boughs over him, the rank grass extended on all sides, not a living being crossed his path, all was silent and still and the scene was like a dull and dreary dream of the land of oblivion. He wandered like a forgotten ghost that had passed into the land of spirits, without yet meeting one of his kind with whom to hold converse.

The condition of a man lost in the woods is one of the most perplexing that can be imagined by a person who has not himself been in a like predicament. Every object he sees, he at first thinks he recognises, and while his whole mind is bent on searching for more that may gradually lead to his extrication, he goes on committing greater errors the farther he proceeds. This was the case with the live-oaker. The sun was now setting with a fiery aspect, and by degrees it sunk in its full circular form, as if giving warning of a sultry morrow. Myriads of insects, delighted at its departure, now filled the air on buzzing wings. Each piping frog arose from the muddy pool in which it had concealed itself; the squirrel retired to its hole, the crow to its roost, and, far above, the harsh croaking voice of the heron announced that, full of anxiety, it was wending its way to the miry interior of some distant swamp. Now the woods began to resound to the shrill cries of the owl; and the breeze, as it swept among the columnar stems of the forest-trees, came laden with heavy and chilling dews. Alas, no moon with her silvery light shone on the dreary scene, and the Lost One, wearied and vexed, laid himself down on the damp ground. Prayer is always consolatory to a man in every difficulty or danger, and the woodsman fervently prayed to his Maker, wished his family a happier night than it was his lot to experience, and with a feverish anxiety waited the return of day.

You may imagine the length of that cold, dull, moonless night. With the dawn of day came the usual fogs of those latitudes. The poor man started on his feet, and with a sorrowful heart, pursued a course which he thought might lead him to some familiar object, although, indeed, he scarcely knew what he was doing. No longer had he the trace of a track to guide him, and yet, as the sun rose, he calculated the many hours of day-light he had before him, and the farther he went continued to walk the faster. But vain were all his hopes: that day was spent in fruitless endeavours to regain the path that led to his home, and when night again approached, the terror that had been gradually spreading over his mind, together with the nervous debility induced by fatigue, anxiety, and hunger, rendered him almost frantic. He told me that at this moment he beat his breast, tore his hair, and, had it not been for the piety with which his parents had in early life imbued his mind, and which had become habitual, would have cursed his existence. Famished as he now was he laid himself on the ground, and fed on the weeds and grass that grew around him. That night was spent in the greatest agony and terror. "I knew my situation," he said to me. "I was fully aware that unless Almighty God came to my assistance, I must perish in those uninhabited woods. I knew that I had walked more than fifty miles, although I had not met with a brook, from which I could quench my thirst, or even allay the burning heat of my parched lips and blood-shot eyes. I knew that if I should not meet with some stream I must die, for my axe was my only weapon, and although deer and bears now and then started within a few yards or even feet of me, not one of them could I kill; and although I was in the midst of abundance, not a mouthful did I expect to procure, to satisfy the cravings of my empty stomach. Sir, may God preserve you from ever feeling as I did the whole of that day!"

For several days after, no one can imagine the condition in which he was, for when he related to me this painful adventure, he assured me that he had lost all recollection of what had happened. "God," he continued, "must have taken pity on me one day, for, as I ran wildly through those dreadful pine barrens, I met with a tortoise. I gazed upon it with amazement and delight, and, although I knew that were I to follow it undisturbed, it would lead me to some water, my hunger and thirst would not allow me to refrain from satisfying both, by eating its flesh, and drinking its blood. With one stroke of my axe the beast was cut in two, and in a few moments I dispatched all but the shell. Oh, Sir, how much I thanked God, whose kindness had put the tortoise in my way! I felt greatly renewed. I sat down at the foot of a pine, gazed on the heavens, thought of my poor wife and children, and again, and again thanked my God for my life, for now I felt less distracted in mind, and more assured that before long I must recover my way, and get back to my home."

The Lost One remained and passed the night, at the foot of the same tree under which his repast had been made. Refreshed by a sound sleep, he started at dawn to resume his weary march. The sun rose bright, and he followed the direction of the shadows. Still the dreariness of the woods was the same, and he was on the point of giving up in despair, when he observed a racoon lying squatted in the grass. Raising his axe, he drove it with such violence through the helpless animal, that it expired without a struggle. What he had done with the turtle, he now did with the racoon, the greater part of which he actually devoured at one meal. With more comfortable feelings, he then resumed his wanderings—his journey I cannot say,—for although in the possession of all his faculties, and in broad daylight, he was worse off than a lame man groping his way in the dark out of a dungeon, of which he knew not where the door stood.

Days, one after another, passed–nay, weeks in succession. He fed now on cabbage-trees, then on frogs and snakes. All that fell in his way was welcome and savoury. Yet he became daily more emaciated, until at length he could scarcely crawl. Forty days had elapsed, by his own reckoning, when he at last reached the banks of the river. His clothes in tatters, his once bright axe dimmed with rust, his face begrimed with beard, his hair matted, and his feeble frame little better than a skeleton covered with parchment, there he laid himself down to die. Amid the perturbed dreams of his fevered fancy, he thought he heard the noise of oars far away on the silent river. He listened, but the sounds died away on his ear. It was indeed a dream, the last glimmer of expiring hope, and now the light of life was about to be quenched for ever. But again, the sound of oars awoke him from his lethargy. He listened so eagerly, that the hum of a fly could not have escaped his ear. They were indeed the measured beats of oars, and now, joy to the forlorn soul! the sound of human voices thrilled to his heart, and awoke the tumultuous pulses of returning hope. On his knees did the eye of God see that poor man by the broad still stream that glittered in the sunbeams, and human eyes soon saw him too, for round that headland covered with tangled brush-wood boldly advances the little boat, propelled by its lusty rowers. The Lost One raises his feeble voice on high;–it was a loud shrill scream of joy and fear. The rowers pause, and look around. Another, but feebler scream, and they observe him. It comes,–his heart flutters, his sight is dimmed, his brain reels, he gasps for breath. It comes,–it has run upon the beach, and the Lost One is found.

This is no tale of fiction, but the relation of an actual occurrence, which might be embellished, no doubt, but which is better in the plain garb of truth. The notes by which I recorded it were written, in the cabin of the once lost live-oaker, about four years after the painful incident occurred. His amiable wife, and loving children, were present at the recital, and never shall I forget the tears that flowed from them as they listened to it, albeit it had long been more familiar to them than a tale thrice told. Sincerely do I wish, good reader, that neither you nor I may ever elicit such sympathy, by having undergone such sufferings, although no doubt such sympathy would be a rich recompense for them.

It only remains for me to say, that the distance between the cabin and the live-oak hummock to which the woodsman was bound, scarcely exceeded 8 miles, while the part of the river at which he was found, was 38 miles from his house. Calculating his daily wanderings at 10 miles, we may believe that they amounted in all to 400. He must, therefore, have rambled in a circuitous direction, which people generally do in such circumstances. Nothing but the great strength of his constitution, and the merciful aid of his Maker, could have supported him for so long a time.

TO BUILD a FIRE

JACK LONDON

Jack London, a writer renowned for his realistic novels of adventure, was equally effective as an author of short stories. The following one is taken from LOST FACE, *published by the Macmillan Company in 1910. It tells how a tenderfoot froze to death when he undertook a long journey alone in weather seventy-five degrees below zero with all the nonchalance of a man going down to the corner for groceries. "To Build a Fire" is an excellent example of London's uncanny ability to convey the feelings and instincts of animals as well as the thoughts of men.*

Day had broken cold and gray, exceedingly cold and gray, when the man turned aside from the main Yukon trail and climbed the high earth-bank, where a dim and little-travelled trail led eastward through the fat spruce timberland. It was a steep bank, and he paused for breath at the top, excusing the act to himself by looking at his watch. It was nine o'clock. There was no sun nor hint of sun, though there was not a cloud in the sky. It was a clear day, and yet there seemed an intangible pall over the face of things, a subtle gloom that made the day dark, and that was due to the absence of sun. This fact did not worry the man. He was used to the lack of sun. It had been days since he had seen the sun, and he knew that a few more days must pass before that cheerful orb, due south, would just peep above the sky-line and dip immediately from view.

The man flung a look back along the way he had come. The Yukon lay a mile wide and hidden under three feet of ice. On top of this ice were as many feet of snow. It was all pure white, rolling in gentle undulations where the ice-jams of the freeze-up had formed. North and south, as far as his eye could see, it was unbroken white, save for a dark hair-line that curved and twisted from around the spruce-covered island to the south, and that curved and twisted away into the north, where it disappeared behind another spruce-covered island. This dark hair-line was the trail—the main trail—that led south five hundred miles to the Chilcoot Pass, Dyea, and salt water; and that led north seventy miles to Dawson, and still on to the north a thousand miles to Nulato, and finally to St. Michael on Bering Sea, a thousand miles and half a thousand more.

But all this—the mysterious, far-reaching hair-line trail, the absence of sun from the sky, the tremendous cold, and the strangeness and weirdness of it all—made no impression on the man. It was not because he was long used to it. He was a newcomer in the land, a *chechaquo*, and this was his first winter. The trouble with him was that he was without imagination. He was quick and alert in the things of life, but only in the things, and not in the significances. Fifty degrees below zero meant eighty-odd degrees of frost. Such fact impressed him as being cold and uncomfortable, and that was all. It did not lead him to meditate upon his frailty as a creature of temperature, and upon man's frailty in general, able only to live within certain narrow limits of heat and cold; and from there on it did not lead him to the conjectural field of immortality and man's place in the universe. Fifty degrees below zero stood for a bite of frost that hurt and that must be guarded against by the use of mittens, ear-flaps, warm moccasins, and thick socks. Fifty degrees below zero was to him just precisely fifty degrees below zero. That there should be anything more to it than that was a thought that never entered his head.

As he turned to go on, he spat speculatively. There was a sharp, explosive crackle that startled him. He spat again. And again, in the air, before it could fall to the snow, the spittle crackled. He knew that at fifty below spittle crackled on the snow, but this spittle had crackled in the air. Undoubtedly it was colder than fifty below—how much colder he did not know. But the temperature did not matter. He was bound for the old claim on the left fork of Henderson Creek, where the boys were already. They had come over across the divide from the Indian Creek country, while he had come the roundabout way to take a look at the possibilities of getting out logs in the spring from the islands in the Yukon. He would be in to camp by six o'clock; a bit after dark, it was true, but the boys would be there, a fire would be going, and a hot supper would be ready. As for lunch, he pressed his hand against the protruding bundle under his jacket. It was also under his shirt, wrapped up in a handkerchief and lying against the naked skin. It was the only way to keep the biscuits from freezing. He smiled agreeably to himself as he thought of those biscuits, each cut open and sopped in bacon grease, and each enclosing a generous slice of fried bacon.

He plunged in among the big spruce trees. The trail was faint. A foot of snow had fallen since the last sled had passed over, and he was glad he was without a sled, travelling light. In fact, he carried nothing but the lunch wrapped in the handkerchief. He was surprised, however, at the cold. It certainly was cold, he concluded, as he rubbed his numb nose and cheek-bones with his mittened hand. He was a warm-whiskered man, but the hair on his face did not protect the high cheek-bones and the eager nose that thrust itself aggressively into the frosty air.

At the man's heels trotted a dog, a big native husky, the proper wolf-dog, gray-coated and without any visible or temperamental difference from its brother, the wild wolf. The animal was depressed by the tremendous cold. It knew that it was no time for travelling. Its instinct told it a truer tale than was told to the man by the man's judgment. In reality, it was not merely colder than fifty below zero; it was colder than sixty below, than seventy below. It was seventy-five below zero. Since the freezing-point is thirty-two above zero, it meant that one hundred and seven degrees of frost obtained. The dog did not know anything about thermometers. Possibly in its brain there was no sharp consciousness of a condition of very cold such as was in the man's brain. But the brute had its instinct. It experienced a vague but menacing apprehension that subdued it and made it slink along at the man's heels, and that made it question eagerly every unwonted movement of the man as if expecting him to go into camp or to seek shelter somewhere and build a fire. The dog had learned fire, and it wanted fire, or else to burrow under the snow and cuddle its warmth away from the air.

The frozen moisture of its breathing had settled on its fur in a fine powder of frost, and especially were its jowls, muzzle, and eyelashes whitened by its crystalled breath. The man's red beard and mustache were likewise frosted, but more solidly, the deposit taking the form of ice and increasing with every warm, moist breath he exhaled. Also, the man was chewing tobacco, and the muzzle of ice held his lips so rigidly that he was unable to clear his chin when he expelled the juice. The result was that a crystal beard of the color and solidity of amber was increasing its length on his chin. If he fell down it would shatter itself, like glass, into brittle fragments. But he did not mind the appendage. It was the penalty all tobacco-chewers paid in that country, and he had been out before in two cold snaps. They had not been so cold as this, he knew, but by the spirit thermometer at Sixty Mile he knew they had been registered at fifty below and at fifty-five.

He held on through the level stretch of woods for several miles, crossed a wide flat of niggerheads, and dropped down a bank to the frozen bed of a small stream. This was Henderson Creek, and he knew he was ten miles from the forks. He looked at his watch. It was ten o'clock. He was making four miles an hour, and he calculated that he would arrive at the forks at half-past twelve. He decided to celebrate that event by eating his lunch there.

The dog dropped in again at his heels, with a tail drooping discouragement, as the man swung along the creek-bed. The furrow of the old sled-trail was plainly visible, but a dozen inches of snow covered the marks of the last runners. In a month no man had come up or down that silent creek. The man held steadily on. He was not much given to thinking, and just then particularly he had nothing to think about save that he would eat lunch at the forks and that at six o'clock he would be in camp with the boys. There was nobody to talk to; and, had there been, speech would have been impossible because of the ice-muzzle on his mouth. So he continued monotonously to chew tobacco and to increase the length of his amber beard.

Once in a while the thought reiterated itself that it was very cold and that he had never experienced such cold. As he walked along he rubbed his cheek-bones and nose with the back of his mittened hand. He did this automatically, now and again changing hands. But rub as he would, the instant he stopped his cheek-bones went numb, and the following instant the end of his nose went numb. He was sure to frost his cheeks; he knew that, and experienced a pang of regret that he had not devised a nose-strap of the sort Bud wore in cold snaps. Such a strap passed across the cheeks, as well, and saved them. But it didn't matter much, after all. What were frosted cheeks? A bit painful, that was all; they were never serious.

Empty as the man's mind was of thoughts, he was keenly observant, and he noticed the changes in the creek, the curves and bends and timber-jams, and always he sharply noted where he placed his feet. Once, coming around a bend, he shied abruptly, like a startled horse, curved away from the place where he had been walking, and retreated several paces back along the trail. The creek he knew was frozen clear to the bottom,—no creek could contain water in that arctic winter,—but he knew also that there were springs that bubbled out from the hillsides and ran along under the snow and on top of the ice of the creek. He knew that the coldest snaps never froze these springs, and he knew likewise their danger. They were traps. They hid pools of water under the snow that might be three inches deep, or three feet. Sometimes a skin of ice half an inch thick covered them, and in turn was covered by the snow. Sometimes there were alternate layers of water and ice-skin, so that when one broke through he kept on breaking through for a while, sometimes wetting himself to the waist.

That was why he had shied in such panic. He had felt the give under his feet and heard the crackle of a snow-hidden ice-skin. And to get his feet wet in such a temperature meant trouble and danger. At the very least it meant delay, for he would be forced to stop and build a fire, and under its protection to bare his feet while he dried his socks and moccasins. He stood and studied the creek-bed and its banks, and decided that the flow of water came from the right. He reflected awhile, rubbing his nose and cheeks, then skirted to the left, stepping gingerly and testing the footing for each step. Once clear of the danger, he took a fresh chew of tobacco and swung along at his four-mile gait.

In the course of the next two hours he came upon several similar traps. Usually the snow above the hidden pools had a sunken, candied appearance that advertised the danger. Once again, however, he had a close call; and once, suspecting danger, he compelled the dog to go on in front. The dog did not want to go. It hung back until the man shoved it forward, and then it went quickly across the white, unbroken surface. Suddenly it broke through, floundered to one side, and got away to firmer footing. It had wet its forefeet and legs, and almost immediately the water that clung to it turned to ice. It made quick efforts to lick the ice off its legs, then dropped down in the snow and began to bite out the ice that had formed between the toes. This was a matter of instinct. To permit the ice to remain would mean sore feet. It did not know this. It merely obeyed the mysterious prompting that arose from the deep crypts of its being. But the man knew, having achieved a judgment on the subject, and he removed the mitten from his right hand and helped tear out the ice-particles. He did not expose his fingers more than a minute, and was astonished at the swift numbness that smote them. It certainly was cold. He pulled on the mitten hastily, and beat the hand savagely across his chest.

At twelve o'clock the day was at its brightest. Yet the sun was too far south on its winter journey to clear the horizon. The bulge of the earth intervened between it and Henderson Creek, where the man walked under a clear sky at noon and cast no shadow. At half-past twelve, to the minute, he arrived at the forks of the creek. He was pleased at the speed he had made. If he kept it up, he would certainly be with the boys by six. He unbuttoned his jacket and shirt and drew forth his lunch. The action consumed no more than a quarter of a minute, yet in that brief moment the numbness laid hold of the exposed fingers. He did not put the mitten on, but, instead, struck the fingers a dozen sharp smashes against his leg. Then he sat down on a snow-covered log to eat. The sting that followed upon the striking of his fingers against his leg ceased so quickly that he was startled. He had had no chance to take a bite of biscuit. He struck the fingers repeatedly and returned them to the mitten, baring the other hand for the purpose of eating. He tried to take a mouthful, but the ice-muzzle prevented. He had forgotten to build a fire and thaw out. He chuckled at his foolishness, and as he chuckled he noted the numbness creeping into the exposed fingers. Also, he noted that the stinging which had first come to his toes when he sat down was already passing away. He wondered whether the toes were warm or numb. He moved them inside the moccasins and decided that they were numb.

He pulled the mitten on hurriedly and stood up. He was a bit frightened. He stamped up and down until the stinging returned into the feet. It certainly was cold, was his thought. That man from Sulphur Creek had spoken the truth when telling how cold it sometimes got in the country. And he had laughed at him at the time! That showed one must not be too sure of things. There was no mistake about it, it *was* cold. He strode up and down, stamping his feet and threshing his arms, until reassured by the returning warmth. Then he got out matches and proceeded to make a fire. From the undergrowth, where high water of the previous spring had lodged a supply of seasoned twigs, he got his fire-wood. Working carefully from a small beginning, he soon had a roaring fire, over which he thawed the ice from his face and in the protection of which he ate his biscuits. For the moment the cold of space was outwitted. The dog took satisfaction in the fire, stretching out close enough for warmth and far enough away to escape being singed.

When the man had finished, he filled his pipe and took his comfortable time over a smoke. Then he pulled on his mittens, settled the ear-flaps of his cap firmly about his ears, and took the creek trail up the left fork. The dog was disappointed and yearned back toward the fire. This man did not know cold. Possibly all the generations of his ancestry had been ignorant of cold, of real cold, of cold one hundred and seven degrees below freezing-point. But the dog knew; all its ancestry knew, and it had inherited the knowledge. And it knew that it was not good to walk abroad in such fearful cold. It was the time to lie snug in a hole in the snow and wait for a curtain of cloud to be drawn across the face of outer space whence this cold came. On the other hand, there was no keen intimacy between the dog and the man. The one was the toil-slave of the other, and the only caresses it had ever received were the caresses of the whip-lash and of harsh and menacing throat-sounds that threatened the whip-lash. So the dog made no effort to communicate its apprehension to the man. It was not concerned in the welfare of the man; it was for its own sake that it yearned back toward the fire. But the man whistled, and spoke to it with the sound of whip-lashes, and the dog swung in at the man's heels and followed after.

The man took a chew of tobacco and proceeded to start a new amber beard. Also, his moist breath quickly powdered with white his mustache, eyebrows, and lashes. There did not seem to be so many springs on the left fork of the Henderson, and for half an hour the man saw no signs of any. And then it happened. At a place where there were no signs, where the soft, unbroken snow seemed to advertise solidity beneath, the man broke through. It was not deep. He wet himself halfway to the knees before he floundered out to the firm crust.

He was angry, and cursed his luck aloud. He had hoped to get into camp with the boys at six o'clock, and this would delay him an hour, for he would have to build a fire and dry out his foot-gear. This was imperative at that low temperature—he knew that much; and he turned aside to the bank, which he climbed. On top, tangled in the underbrush about the trunks of several small spruce trees, was a high-water deposit of dry fire-wood—sticks and twigs, principally, but also larger portions of seasoned branches and fine, dry, last-year's grasses. He threw down several large pieces on top of the snow. This served for a foundation and prevented the young flame from drowning itself in the snow it otherwise would melt. The flame he got by touching a match to a small shred of birch-bark that he took from his pocket. This burned even more readily than paper. Placing it on the foundation, he fed the young flame with wisps of dry grass and with the tiniest dry twigs.

He worked slowly and carefully, keenly aware of his danger. Gradually, as the flame grew stronger, he increased the size of the twigs with which he fed it. He squatted in the snow, pulling the twigs out from their entanglement in the brush and feeding directly to the flame. He knew there must be no failure. When it is seventy-five below zero, a man must not fail in his first attempt to build a fire—that is, if his feet are wet. If his feet are dry, and he fails, he can run along the trail for half a mile and restore his circulation. But the circulation of wet and freezing feet cannot be restored by running when it is seventy-five below. No matter how fast he runs, the wet feet will freeze the harder.

All this the man knew. The old-timer on Sulphur Creek had told him about it the previous fall, and now he was appreciating the advice. Already all sensation had gone out of his feet. To build the fire he had been forced to remove his mittens, and the fingers had quickly gone numb. His pace of four miles an hour had kept his heart pumping blood to the surface of his body and to all the extremities. But the instant he stopped, the action of the pump eased down. The cold of space smote the unprotected tip of the planet, and he, being on that unprotected tip, received the full force of the blow. The blood of his body recoiled before it. The blood was alive, like the dog, and like the dog it wanted to hide away and cover itself up from the fearful cold. So long as he walked four miles an hour, he pumped that blood, willy-nilly, to the surface; but now it ebbed away and sank down into the recesses of his body. The extremities were the first to feel its absence. His wet feet froze the faster, and his exposed fingers numbed the faster, though they had not yet begun to freeze. Nose and cheeks were already freezing, while the skin of all his body chilled as it lost its blood.

But he was safe. Toes and nose and cheeks would be only touched by the frost, for the fire was beginning to burn with strength. He was feeding it with twigs the size of his finger. In another minute he would be able to feed it with branches the size of his wrist, and then he could remove his wet foot-gear, and, while it dried, he could keep his naked feet warm by the fire, rubbing them at first, of course, with snow. The fire was a success. He was safe. He remembered the advice of the old-timer on Sulphur Creek, and smiled. The old-timer had been very serious in laying down the law that no man must travel alone in the Klondike after fifty below. Well, here he was; he had had the accident; he was alone; and he had saved himself. Those old-timers were rather womanish, some of them, he thought. All a man had to do was to keep his head, and he was all right. Any man who was a man could travel alone. But it was surprising, the rapidity with which his cheeks and nose were freezing. And he had not thought his fingers could go lifeless in so short a time. Lifeless they were, for he could scarcely make them move together to grip a twig, and they seemed remote from his body and from him. When he touched a twig, he had to look and see whether or not he had hold of it. The wires were pretty well down between him and his finger-ends.

All of which counted for little. There was the fire, snapping and crackling and promising life with every dancing flame. He started to untie his moccasins. They were coated with ice; the thick German socks were like sheaths of iron halfway to the knees; and the moccasin strings were like rods of steel all twisted and knotted as by some conflagration. For a moment he tugged with his numb fingers, then, realizing the folly of it, he drew his sheath-knife.

But before he could cut the strings, it happened. It was his own fault or, rather, his mistake. He should not have built the fire under the spruce tree. He should have built it in the open. But it had been easier to pull the twigs from the brush and drop them directly on the fire. Now the tree under which he had done this carried a weight of snow on its boughs. No wind had blown for weeks, and each bough was fully freighted. Each time he had pulled a twig he had communicated a slight agitation to the tree —an imperceptible agitation, so far as he was concerned, but an agitation sufficient to bring about the disaster. High up in the tree one bough capsized its load of snow. This fell on the boughs beneath, capsizing them. This process continued, spreading out and involving the whole tree. It grew like an avalanche, and it descended without warning upon the man and the fire, and the fire was blotted out! Where it had burned was a mantle of fresh and disordered snow.

The man was shocked. It was as though he had just heard his own sentence of death. For a moment he sat and stared at the spot where the fire had been. Then he grew very calm. Perhaps the old-timer on Sulphur Creek was right. If he had only had a trail-mate he would have been in no danger now. The trail-mate could have built the fire. Well, it was up to him to build the fire over again, and this second time there must be no failure. Even if he succeeded, he would most likely lose some toes. His feet must be badly frozen by now, and there would be some time before the second fire was ready.

Such were his thoughts, but he did not sit and think them. He was busy all the time they were passing through his mind. He made a new foundation for a fire, this time in the open, where no treacherous tree could blot it out. Next, he gathered dry grasses and tiny twigs from the high-water flotsam. He could not bring his fingers together to pull them out, but he was able to gather them by the handful. In this way he got many rotten twigs and bits of green moss that were undesirable, but it was the best he could do. He worked methodically, even collecting an armful of the larger branches to be used later when the fire gathered strength. And all the while the dog sat and watched him, a certain yearning wistfulness in its eyes, for it looked upon him as the fire-provider, and the fire was slow in coming.

When all was ready, the man reached in his pocket for a second piece of birch-bark. He knew the bark was there, and, though he could not feel it with his fingers, he could hear its crisp rustling as he fumbled for it. Try as he would, he could not clutch hold of it. And all the time, in his consciousness, was the knowledge that each instant his feet were freezing. This thought tended to put him in a panic, but he fought against it and kept calm. He pulled on his mittens with his teeth, and threshed his arms back and forth, beating his hands with all his might against his sides. He did this sitting down, and he stood up to do it; and all the while the dog sat in the snow, its wolf-brush of a tail curled around warmly over its forefeet, its sharp wolf-ears pricked forward intently as it watched the man. And the man, as he beat and threshed with his arms and hands, felt a great surge of envy as he regarded the creature that was warm and secure in its natural covering.

After a time he was aware of the first far-away signals of sensation in his beaten fingers. The faint tingling grew stronger till it evolved into a stinging ache that was excruciating, but which the man hailed with satisfaction. He stripped the mitten from his right hand and fetched forth the birch-bark. The exposed fingers were quickly going numb again. Next he brought out his bunch of sulphur matches. But the tremendous cold had already driven the life out of his fingers. In his effort to separate one match from the others, the whole bunch fell in the snow. He tried to pick it out of the snow, but failed. The dead fingers could neither touch nor clutch. He was very careful. He drove the thought of his freezing feet, and nose, and cheeks, out of his mind, devoting his whole soul to the matches. He watched, using the sense of vision in place of that of touch, and when he saw his fingers on each side the bunch, he closed them—that is, he willed to close them, for the wires were down, and the fingers did not obey. He pulled the mitten on the right hand, and beat it fiercely against his knee. Then, with both mittened hands, he scooped the bunch of matches, along with much snow, into his lap. Yet he was no better off.

After some manipulation he managed to get the bunch between the heels of his mittened hands. In this fashion he carried it to his mouth. The ice crackled and snapped when by a violent effort he opened his mouth. He drew the lower jaw in, curled the upper lip out of the way, and scraped the bunch with his upper teeth in order to separate a match. He succeeded in getting one, which he dropped on his lap. He was no better off. He could not pick it up. Then he devised a way. He picked it up in his teeth and scratched it on his leg. Twenty times he scratched before he succeeded in lighting it. As it flamed he held it with his teeth to the birch-bark. But the burning brimstone went up his nostrils and into his lungs, causing him to cough spasmodically. The match fell into the snow and went out.

The old-timer on Sulphur Creek was right, he thought in the moment of controlled despair that ensued: after fifty below, a man should travel with a partner. He beat his hands, but failed in exciting any sensation. Suddenly he bared both hands, removing the mittens with his teeth. He caught the whole bunch between the heels of his hands. His arm-muscles not being frozen enabled him to press the hand-heels tightly against the matches. Then he scratched the bunch along his leg. It flared into flame, seventy sulphur matches at once! There was no wind to blow them out. He kept his head to one side to escape the strangling fumes, and held the blazing bunch to the birch-bark. As he so held it, he became aware of sensation in his hand. His flesh was burning. He could smell it. Deep down below the surface he could feel it. The sensation developed into pain that grew acute. And still he endured it, holding the flame of the matches clumsily to the bark that would not light readily because his own burning hands were in the way, absorbing most of the flame.

At last, when he could endure no more, he jerked his hands apart. The blazing matches fell sizzling into the snow, but the birch-bark was alight. He began laying dry grasses and the tiniest twigs on the flame. He could not pick and choose, for he had to lift the fuel between the heels of his hands. Small pieces of rotten wood and green moss clung to the twigs, and he bit them off as well as he could with his teeth. He cherished the flame carefully and awkwardly. It meant life, and it must not perish. The withdrawal of blood from the surface of his body now made him begin to shiver, and he grew more awkward. A large piece of green moss fell squarely on the little fire. He tried to poke it out with his fingers, but his shivering frame made him poke too far, and he disrupted the nucleus of the little fire, the burning grasses and tiny twigs separating and scattering. He tried to poke them together again, but in spite of the tenseness of the effort, his shivering got away with him, and the twigs were hopelessly scattered. Each twig gushed a puff of smoke and went out. The fire-provider had failed. As he looked apathetically about him, his eyes chanced on the dog, sitting across the ruins of the fire from him, in the snow, making restless, hunching movements, slightly lifting one forefoot and then the other, shifting its weight back and forth on them with wistful eagerness.

The sight of the dog put a wild idea into his head. He remembered the tale of the man, caught in a blizzard, who killed a steer and crawled inside the carcass, and so was saved. He would kill the dog and bury his hands in the warm body until the numbness went out of them. Then he could build another fire. He spoke to the dog, calling it to him; but in his voice was a strange note of fear that frightened the animal, who had never known the man to speak in such way before. Something was the matter, and its suspicious nature sensed danger—it knew not what danger, but somewhere, somehow, in its brain arose an apprehension of the man. It flattened its ears down at the sound of the man's voice, and its restless, hunching movements and the liftings and shiftings of its fore-feet became more pronounced; but it would not come to the man. He got on his hands and knees and crawled toward the dog. This unusual posture again excited suspicion, and the animal sidled mincingly away.

The man sat up in the snow for a moment and struggled for calmness. Then he pulled on his mittens, by means of his teeth, and got upon his feet. He glanced down at first in order to assure himself that he was really standing up, for the absence of sensation in his feet left him unrelated to the earth. His erect position in itself started to drive the webs of suspicion from the dog's mind; and when he spoke peremptorily, with the sound of whip-lashes in his voice, the dog rendered its customary allegiance and came to him. As it came within reaching distance, the man lost his control. His arms flashed out to the dog, and he experienced genuine surprise when he discovered that his hands could not clutch, that there was neither bend nor feeling in his fingers. He had forgotten for the moment that they were frozen and that they were freezing more and more. All this happened quickly, and before the animal could get away, he encircled its body with his arms. He sat down in the snow, and in this fashion held the dog, while it snarled and whined and struggled.

But it was all he could do, hold its body encircled in his arms and sit there. He realized that he could not kill the dog. There was no way to do it. With his helpless hands he could neither draw nor hold his sheath-knife nor throttle the animal. He released it, and it plunged wildly away, with tail between its legs, and still snarling. It halted forty feet away and surveyed him curiously, with ears sharply pricked forward. The man looked down at his hands in order to locate them, and found them hanging on the ends of his arms. It struck him as curious that one should have to use his eyes in order to find out where his hands were. He began threshing his arms back and forth, beating the mittened hands against his sides. He did this for five minutes, violently, and his heart pumped enough blood up to the surface to put a stop to his shivering. But no sensation was aroused in the hands. He had an impression that they hung like weights on the ends of his arms but when he tried to run the impression down, he could not find it.

A certain fear of death, dull and oppressive, came to him. This fear quickly became poignant as he realized that it was no longer a mere matter of freezing his fingers and toes, or of losing his hands and feet, but that it was a matter of life and death with the chances against him. This threw him into a panic, and he turned and ran up the creek-bed along the old, dim trail. The dog joined in behind and kept up with him. He ran blindly, without intention, in fear such as he had never known in his life. Slowly, as he ploughed and floundered through the snow, he began to see things again,—the banks of the creek, the old timber-jams, the leafless aspens, and the sky. The running made him feel better. He did not shiver. Maybe, if he ran on, his feet would thaw out; and, anyway, if he ran far enough, he would reach camp and the boys. Without doubt he would lose some fingers and toes and some of his face; but the boys would take care of him, and save the rest of him when he got there. And at the same time there was another thought in his mind that said he would never get to the camp and the boys; that it was too many miles away, that the freezing had too great a start on him, and that he would soon be stiff and dead. This thought he kept in the background and refused to consider. Sometimes it pushed itself forward and demanded to be heard, but he thrust it back and strove to think of other things.

It struck him as curious that he could run at all on feet so frozen that he could not feel them when they struck the earth and took the weight of his body. He seemed to himself to skim along above the surface, and to have no connection with the earth. Somewhere he had once seen a winged Mercury, and he wondered if Mercury felt as he felt when skimming over the earth.

His theory of running until he reached camp and the boys had one flaw in it: he lacked the endurance. Several times he stumbled, and finally he tottered, crumbled up and fell. When he tried to rise, he failed. He must sit and rest, he decided, and next time he would merely walk and keep on going. As he sat and regained his breath, he noted that he was feeling quite warm and comfortable. He was not shivering, and it even seemed that a warm glow had come to his chest and trunk. And yet, when he touched his nose or cheeks, there was no sensation. Running would not thaw them out. Nor would it thaw out his hands and feet. Then the thought came to him that the frozen portions of his body must be extending. He tried to keep this thought down, to forget it, to think of something else; he was aware of the panicky feeling that it caused, and he was afraid of the panic. But the thought asserted itself, and persisted, until it produced a vision of his body totally frozen. This was too much, and he made another wild run along the trail. Once he slowed down to a walk, but the thought of the freezing extending itself made him run again.

And all the time the dog ran with him, at his heels. When he fell down a second time, it curled its tail over its forefeet and sat in front of him, facing him, curiously eager and intent. The warmth and security of the animal angered him, and he cursed it till it flattened down its ears appeasingly. This time the shivering came more quickly upon the man. He was losing in his battle with the frost. It was creeping into his body from all sides. The thought of it drove him on, but he ran no more than a hundred feet, when he staggered and pitched headlong. It was his last panic. When he had recovered his breath and control, he sat up and entertained in his mind the conception of meeting death with dignity. However, the conception did not come to him in such terms. His idea of it was that he had been making a fool of himself, running around like a chicken with its head cut off—such was the simile that occurred to him. Well, he was bound to freeze anyway, and he might as well take it decently. With this new-found peace of mind came the first glimmerings of drowsiness. A good idea, he thought, to sleep off to death. It was like taking an anaesthetic. Freezing was not so bad as people thought. There were lots worse ways to die.

He pictured the boys finding his body next day. Suddenly he found himself with them, coming along the trail and looking for himself. And, still with them, he came around a turn in the trail and found himself lying in the snow. He did not belong with himself any more, for even then he was out of himself, standing with the boys and looking at himself in the snow.

It certainly was cold, was his thought. When he got back to the States he could tell the folks what real cold was. He drifted on from this to a vision of the old-timer on Sulphur Creek. He could see him quite clearly, warm and comfortable, and smoking a pipe.

"You were right, old hoss; you were right," the man mumbled to the old-timer of Sulphur Creek.

Then the man drowsed off into what seemed to him the most comfortable and satisfying sleep he had ever known. The dog sat facing him and waiting. The brief day drew to a close in a long, slow twilight. There were no signs of a fire to be made, and, besides, never in the dog's experience had it known a man to sit like that in the snow and make no fire. As the twilight drew on, its eager yearning for the fire mastered it, and with a great lifting and shifting of forefeet, it whined softly, then flattened its ears down in anticipation of being chidden by the man. But the man remained silent. Later, the dog whined loudly. And still later it crept close to the man and caught the scent of death. This made the animal bristle and back away. A little longer it delayed, howling under the stars that leaped and danced and shone brightly in the cold sky. Then it turned and trotted up the trail in the direction of the camp it knew, where were the other food-providers and fire-providers.

PART II

Nature Transformed by Poets, Bards, and Yarn-Spinners

THE STAG WHO SPROUTED a CHERRY TREE

RUDOLPH ERICH RASPE

—a selection from BARON MÜNCHAUSEN *(1785), by Rudolph Erich Raspe.*
Baron Münchausen, an aristocrat of Gottingen, had a reputation as a teller of improbable, exaggerated tales. However, the stories published under his name were actually written by Rudolph Erich Raspe, a professor of archeology, and himself an outrageous liar and swindler. Some of the most amusing of the Münchausen stories concern his hunting experiences.

You have heard, I dare say, of the hunter's and sportsman's saint and protector, St. Hubert, and of the noble stag which appeared to him in the forest, with the holy cross between his antlers. I have paid my homage to that saint every year in good fellowship, and seen this stag a thousand times, either painted in churches or embroidered in the stars of his knights; so that, upon the honour and conscience of a good sportsman, I hardly know whether there may not have been formerly, or whether there are not such crossed stags even at this present day. But let me rather tell what I have seen myself. Having one day spent all my shot, I found myself unexpectedly in presence of a stately stag, looking at me as unconcernedly as if he had known of my empty pouches. I charged immediately with powder, and upon it a good handful of cherry-stones for I had sucked the fruit as far as the hurry would permit. Thus I let fly at him, and hit him just on the middle of the forehead, between his antlers. It stunned him, he staggered, yet he made off. A year or two after, being with a party in that same forest, I beheld a noble stag with a fine full-grown cherry-tree, above ten feet high, between his antlers. I immediately recollected my former adventure, looked upon him as my property, and brought him to the ground by one shot, which at once gave me the haunch and cherry sauce; for the tree was covered with the richest fruit, the like I had never tasted before. Who knows but some passionate holy sportsman, or sporting abbot, or bishop, may have shot, planted, and fixed the cross between the antlers of St. Hubert's stag, in a manner similar to this? In a case of distress or dilemma, which too often happens to keen sportsmen, one is apt to grasp at anything for safety, and to try any expedient, rather than miss the favourable opportunity. I have many times found myself in that trying situation.

THE KINGDOM of KANSAS

JAMES STEVENS

—a selection from PAUL BUNYAN *by James Stevens, 2nd ed., New York: Alfred A. Knopf, Inc., 1948.*

The Paul Bunyan stories probably had their origin in the legendary exploits of a fighter named Paul Bunyon who took part in a rebellion of French-Canadians against the English crown in 1837. He later became a logger. Lumberjacks south of the Canadian border Americanized both the hero's name and his character. As James Stevens remarks, "it is simple . . . to imagine the Americans 'improving' on the first stories about Paul Bunyon, only to ridicule his extravagant admirers; and then developing their own Paul Bunyan legend to ease their weariness when their twelve-hour day was done."

In the Paul Bunyan stories, not only are the human characters legendary, but nature herself. Everything in these tales is larger than life-size, and there is no limit to their invention.

No region of Real America, save Kansas, boasted of its weather in Paul Bunyan's time. In the heyday of the mighty logger the climates and seasons were not systematized; they came and went and behaved without rule or reason. There were many years with two winters, and sometimes all four seasons would come and go in one month. The wind would frequently blow straight up and then straight down. Sometimes it would simply stand still and blow in one place. In its most prankish moods it would blow all ways at once. The weather was indeed powerful strange in those days and it got itself talked about. And nowhere were its ways more evil than in Utah.

When Paul Bunyan moved his camp to the state of Utah

for the purpose of logging off its forests of stonewood trees he was not careless of the climate; he merely failed to suspect its treachery. Besides, other troubles beset him. The gritty texture of the stonewood timber dulled the edge of an ax bit in two strokes. At the end of their twelve-hour day in the woods the loggers had to sharpen axes for seven hours. They were always fagged out. Then there was only one small river near the forests, and Babe, the blue ox, who had got hayfever again since coming West, drank it dry every fifteen minutes. The loggers thirsted, and they were bedeviled by sand in their blankets and in the beans, for every time Babe sneezed he raised a dust storm that rolled its clouds through the cookhouse and the bunkhouses and covered the great plain and the hills around the camp. A spirit of dark and evil melancholy settled on the loggers.

Paul Bunyan hoped for an adequate water supply from the December snows. And he brought all his inventive powers to the problem of felling the stonewood trees. In eleven days and nights he devised eight hundred and five systems, machines and implements, and from this galaxy he selected a noble tool.

Paul Bunyan's new invention was the double-bitted ax, which is used everywhere in the woods to-day. Paul Bunyan devised it so that a faller could chop with one blade, then twist the handle and whet the other blade on the gritty stonewood with the backward swing.

But even with the new axes the logging went on slowly. The camp supply of elbow grease gave out, and the loggers suffered stiffened joints. The December snows were light, and the thirsty blue ox continued to drink the entire water supply. The bunkhouses came to be dens of ominous brooding and quiet instead of gay and noisy habitations. Finally the shipment of webfooted turkeys from the Great Lakes arrived too late for Christmas dinner. The loggers became dour, gaunt, embittered men.

Then came New Year's Day and outrageous fortune. When the loggers went to work at the first thinning of darkness they attributed the peculiar oppressive warmth of the morning to an unusual Chinook wind. There was, however, no wind at all. Then the rising sun shot blazing rays into a cloudless sky. Even then the loggers did not realize that they were witnessing an Event. This was the beginning of a notable year, the Year of the Hot Winter. As the sun climbed higher the heat grew more intense. The Christmas snow had vanished at the first burning touch of day. The ground baked and cracked. The stonewood trees glittered in a fierce light. Each logger threw off his mackinaw, muffler, sweater, stagged shirt, woolen overshirt and undershirt, his parrafin pants, mackinaw pants and overalls and his Arctic socks, heavy wool socks, light wool socks and cotton socks. All heavy clothing was speedily thrown aside, and everywhere in the plain, in the valleys, and on the hillsides were piles of garments, and by each pile a logger toiled, clad only in drawers and calked boots. But still sweat dripped and trickled from their bodies; they labored more and more languorously. Each quarter of an hour the blue ox, with lolling tongue, dashed madly for the river and drank it dry.

Paul Bunyan was distressed by this change in his affairs, but he was not daunted. Confident that his loggers would do their best in the meanwhile, he again retired to solitude, hoping to devise something that would conquer the hostile and unnatural season. He returned with the great timber scythe, with which he could fell a full section of timber with one swing of his mighty arms. Carrying the timber scythe over his shoulder, Paul Bunyan strode toward his camp. His tread was vigorous despite the deadening heat. Benevolent ideas stirred his heart. He himself would do the arduous labor of felling the stonewood trees; the loggers would be asked only to do the lighter work of trimming and bucking the trees into logs. They were a fine bunch of savages; ordinarily they would not allow even Paul Bunyan to do their natural work. Perhaps they would resist such intrusion now. But the great logger was sure of his persuasive powers.

As he neared the camp, busy as he was with philanthropic thoughts, he failed to note an unusual silence in the woods and about the bunkhouses. Not until he saw Babe and the Big Swede sleeping in the stable was he made aware of the extraordinary. Paul Bunyan went next to the camp office. Johnny Inkslinger, that tower of energy, was sleeping at his desk! His fountain pen had dropped from his hand, and as it was fed by hose lines from twenty-five barrels of ink, a black stream gushed from its point and flooded the floor. A chorus of faint snores came from each bunkhouse. The cookhouse looked gloomy and deserted. In the woods the axes and saws lay where the loggers had left them. For one hundred and seventy-nine minutes Paul Bunyan stood silently in the midst of his camp, tormented by wrath, regret and sorrow. His outfit had failed him. After all these years of comradeship in labor they had allowed a mere hot winter to provoke them into faithlessness. He had left them without an idea that they would be untrue to the job while he was scheming to make it a success. But they had weakened. Very well, he thought, after his brief period of emotion, he would perform their labor for them while they snored. They should awaken to shame.

One stride brought him into the first clearing made among the stonewood trees. Without losing a second, he threw the timber scythe from his shoulder, he grasped its handles, then took a long swing, and the first section of trees thundered to the ground. On he went, making a circular swath. As he stepped with his right foot the sharp scythe blade crashed through the trees on the cutting stroke, and as he stepped with his left he brought the scythe behind him with a vigorous swing. On and on he labored, his steps coming faster as the circle widened. Every seven hours he paused to whet the blade of the timber scythe on a bundle of the stonewood trees which he carried in his hip pocket. The hot winter drove its fires upon him, but his passion of toil repelled them with a stronger flame. The great logger's walk became a run; the dazzling blade of the timber scythe flashed in strokes of inconceivable rapidity; the sections of stonewood trees fell in a steady roar.

Then Paul Bunyan began to sweat. He had labored before this, but never so savagely, nor in such penetrating heat. Only the man who raises a good sweat for the first time can realize what an astounding store of perspiration the human body can hold. On occasion it gushes from innumerable springs, seeming inexhaustible. It streams down the crevices and valleys of the body and floods the flat spaces; it soaks the clothing and drips to the ground. Imagine then what happened when Paul Bunyan's stored perspiration was unloosed. As he toiled on, ever more fiercely, his sweat flooded his boots, it surged over their tops and foamed towards the ground like two Niagaras. His swinging body and flying arms flung out clouds of spray. These strange waters coursed over the plains in torrents and gathered in heaving pools. The little river was submerged, drowned, exterminated. The waters crept towards the camp. Paul Bunyan, more and more engrossed with his labor as time went on, did not note the rising flood. His circle grew wider and wider. It left the plain and swung around the bordering slopes. Section after section of the trees was felled, only to be covered by water, for the stonewood timber was too heavy to float. But Paul Bunyan labored around and around the circle, quite unaware of the tragical consequences of his efforts.

For five days and nights the loggers lay in their bunks, too lazy to get up to eat, too lazy to do aught but drowse and dream. But at twelve o'clock on the fifth night the waters had reached the bunkhouses, and they learned of their peril. Yells of fear arose from every quarter, and in a few moments the whole camp, with the exception of Babe, the Big Swede, and Johnny Inkslinger, was aroused. Fright made the loggers forget the hot winter, and gave them energy. When they looked out on a vast lake glittering in the moonlight, and saw in the dim distance the twin rivers roaring from Paul Bunyan's boots, they knew that speedy and efficient action was necessary to save their lives. The best swimmers swam out to the tool house and brought back hammers, saws and nails. Each logger then began to build a boat from his bunk, and for three hours they worked feverishly and silently constructing the vessels. When the last one was finished the word was passed along and in a few moments the boats, each one carrying a logger and his blankets, swarmed from the bunkhouses. Before the armada had gone twenty feet the boats all filled with water and sank, while the loggers uttered lamentable cries. These changed to sounds of rejoicing, however, when it was discovered that the water was only waist deep. The loggers rescued their bundles from the boats and scampered to the shore like a holiday host at a beach.

But their joy did not last; it quickly gave way to dread. Paul Bunyan, toiling more desperately every moment, was rapidly moving around the circle. In a short time he would be upon them, and at any instant he might discover the fate of his trees, the flooding of his camp, his complete disaster. The loggers all understood the reason for the mighty man's wrathful labor. Their sense of blame confused them and smothered their native courage. The host began to move over the hills, haltingly at first, and with heads bowed like penitents. Then, as the volleying thunder of Paul Bunyan's timber scythe sounded nearer and nearer, they lifted their heads and struck a faster pace. Then guilty fears possessed them and every logger of the lot began to gallop madly. Someone yelled, "Ol' Paul's a comin'!" and the warning cry was echoed from thousands of throats all over the hills. The loggers were taken by panic; the runaway became a stampede. By dawn they were making such running leaps that each logger would hit his chin with his front knee and his head with his back heel at every stride. They were so scared that they never stopped until they got to Kansas.

THE MAN WHO ACTED as the SUN

FRANZ BOAS

Many American Indian legends have something of the freshness of the dawn about them. This is quite natural, because often they explain the beginnings of the world, why animals and men were created to look as they do, and how the seasons came to be.

The following mythological tale is taken from Franz Boas, THE MYTHOLOGY OF THE BELLA COOLA INDIANS, *New York: Publications of the Jesup North Pacific Expedition, 1898, as edited by Stith Thompson in* TALES OF THE NORTH AMERICAN INDIANS, *Cambridge, Mass.: Harvard University Press, 1929.*

Once upon a time there lived a woman* some distance up Bella Coola River. She refused the offer of marriage from the young men of the tribe, because she desired to marry the Sun. She left her village and went to seek the Sun. Finally she reached his house, and married the Sun. After she had been there one day, she had a child. He grew very quickly, and on the second day of his life he was able to walk and to talk. After a short time he said to his mother, "I should like to see your mother and your father"; and he began to cry, making his mother feel homesick. When the Sun saw that his wife felt downcast and that his son was longing to see his grandparents, he said, "You may return to the earth to see your parents. Descend along my eyelashes." His eyelashes were the rays of the Sun, which he extended down to his wife's home, where they lived with the woman's parents.

---

* A number of Indian names have been omitted from this passage. They do not affect the meaning.

The boy was playing with the children of the village, who were teasing him, saying that he had no father. He began to cry, and went to his mother, whom he asked for bow and arrows. His mother gave him what he requested. He went outside and began to shoot his arrows towards the sky. The first arrow struck the sky and stuck in it; the second arrow hit the notch of the first one; and thus he continued until a chain was formed, extending from the sky down to the place where he was standing. Then he ascended the chain. He found the house of the sun, which he entered. He told his father that the boys had been teasing him, and he asked him to let him carry the sun. But his father said, "You cannot do it. I carry many torches. Early in the morning and late in the evening I burn small torches, but at noon I burn the large ones." The boy insisted on his request. Then his father gave him the torches, warning him at the same time to observe carefully the instructions that he was giving him in regard to their use.

Early the next morning, the young man started on the course of the sun, carrying the torches. Soon he grew impatient, and lighted all the torches at once. Then it grew very hot. The trees began to burn, and many animals jumped into the water to save themselves, but the water began to boil. Then his mother covered the people with her blanket, and thus saved them. The animals hid under stones. The ermine crept into a hole, which, however, was not quite large enough, so that the tip of its tail protruded from the entrance. It was scorched, and since that time the tip of the ermine's tail has been black. The mountain-goat hid in a cave, hence its skin is perfectly white. All the animals that did not hide were scorched, and therefore have black skins, but the skin on their lower side remained lighter. When the Sun saw what was happening, he said to his son, "Why do you do so? Do you think it is good that there are no people on the earth?"

The Sun took him and cast him down from the heavens, saying, "You shall be the mink, and future generations of man shall hunt you."

THE WILD WOOD

KENNETH GRAHAME

—a selection from The Wind in the Willows *(1908), by Kenneth Grahame.*

Kenneth Grahame was a Scottish banker and naturalist whose book, The Wind in the Willows, *has, for many years, been beloved by both children and adults. Although he ascribes human traits to his animal characters, he places them in an authentic, natural environment.*

The Mole had long wanted to make the acquaintance of the Badger. He seemed, by all accounts, to be such an important personage and, though rarely visible, to make his unseen influence felt by everybody about the place. But whenever the Mole mentioned his wish to the Water Rat he always found himself put off. 'It's all right,' the Rat would say. 'Badger'll turn up some day or other—he's always turning up—and then I'll introduce you. The best of fellows! But you must not only take him *as* you find him, but *when* you find him.'

'Couldn't you ask him here—dinner or something?' said the Mole.

'He wouldn't come,' replied the Rat simply. 'Badger hates Society, and invitations, and dinner, and all that sort of thing.'

'Well, then, supposing we go and call on *him?*' suggested the Mole.

'O, I'm sure he wouldn't like that at *all,*' said the Rat, quite alarmed. 'He's so very shy, he'd be sure to be offended. I've never even ventured to call on him at his own home myself, though I know him so well. Besides, we can't. It's quite out of the question, because he lives in the very middle of the Wild Wood.'

'Well, supposing he does,' said the Mole. 'You told me the Wild Wood was all right, you know.'

'O, I know, I know, so it is,' replied the Rat evasively. 'But I think we won't go there just now. Not *just* yet. It's a long way, and he wouldn't be at home at this time of year anyhow, and he'll be coming along some day, if you'll wait quietly.'

The Mole had to be content with this. But the Badger never came along, and every day brought its amusements, and it was not till summer was long over, and cold and frost and miry ways kept them much indoors, and the swollen river raced past outside their windows with a speed that mocked at boating of any sort or kind, that he found his thoughts dwelling again with much persistence on the solitary grey Badger, who lived his own life by himself, in his hole in the middle of the Wild Wood.

In the winter time the Rat slept a great deal, retiring early and rising late. During his short day he sometimes scribbled poetry or did other small domestic jobs about the house; and, of course, there were always animals dropping in for a chat, and consequently there was a good deal of story-telling and comparing notes on the past summer and all its doings.

Such a rich chapter it had been, when one came to look back on it all! With illustrations so numerous and so very highly coloured! The pageant of the river bank had marched steadily along, unfolding itself in scene-pictures that succeeded each other in stately procession. Purple loosestrife arrived early, shaking luxuriant tangled locks along the edge of the mirror whence its own face laughed back at it. Willow-herb, tender and wistful, like a pink sunset cloud, was not slow to follow. Comfrey, the purple hand-in-hand with the white, crept forth to take its place in the line; and at last one morning the diffident and delaying dog-rose stepped delicately on the stage, and one knew, as if string-music had announced it in stately chords that strayed into a gavotte, that June at last was here. One member of the company was still awaited; the shepherd-boy for the nymphs to woo, the knight for whom the ladies waited at the window, the prince that was to kiss the sleeping summer back to life and love. But when meadow-sweet, debonair and odorous in amber jerkin, moved graciously to his place in the group, then the play was ready to begin.

And what a play it had been! Drowsy animals, snug in their holes while wind and rain were battering at their doors, recalled still keen mornings, an hour before sunrise, when the white mist, as yet undispersed, clung closely along the surface of the water; then the shock of the early plunge, the scamper along the bank, and the radiant transformation of earth, air, and water, when suddenly the sun was with them again, and grey was gold and colour was born and sprang out of the earth once more. They recalled the languorous siesta of hot mid-day, deep in green undergrowth, the sun striking through in tiny golden shafts and spots; the boating and bathing of the afternoon, the rambles along dusty lanes and through yellow cornfields; and the long, cool evening at last, when so many threads were gathered up, so many friendships rounded, and so many adventures planned for the morrow. There was plenty to talk about on those short winter days when the animals found themselves round the fire; still, the Mole had a good deal of spare time on his hands, and so one afternoon, when the Rat in his arm-chair before the blaze was alternately dozing and trying over rhymes that wouldn't fit, he formed the resolution to go out by himself and explore the Wild Wood, and perhaps strike up an acquaintance with Mr. Badger.

It was a cold still afternoon with a hard steely sky overhead, when he slipped out of the warm parlour into the open air. The country lay bare and entirely leafless around him, and he thought that he had never seen so far and so intimately into the insides of things as on that winter day when Nature was deep in her annual slumber and seemed to have kicked the clothes off. Copses, dells, quarries and all hidden places, which had been mysterious mines for exploration in leafy summer, now exposed themselves and their secrets pathetically, and seemed to ask him to overlook their shabby poverty for a while, till they could riot in rich masquerade as before, and trick and entice him with the old deceptions. It was pitiful in a way, and yet cheering—even exhilarating. He was glad that he liked the country undecorated, hard, and stripped of its finery. He had got down to the bare bones of it, and they were fine and strong and simple. He did not want the warm clover and the play of seeding grasses; the screens of quickset, the billowy drapery of beech and elm seemed best away; and with great cheerfulness of spirit he pushed on towards the Wild Wood, which lay before him low and threatening, like a black reef in some still southern sea.

There was nothing to alarm him at first entry. Twigs crackled under his feet, logs tripped him, funguses on stumps resembled caricatures, and startled him for the moment by their likeness to something familiar and far away; but that was all fun, and exciting. It led him on, and he penetrated to where the light was less, and trees crouched nearer and nearer, and holes made ugly mouths at him on either side.

Everything was very still now. The dusk advanced on him steadily, rapidly, gathering in behind and before; and the light seemed to be draining away like flood-water.

Then the faces began.

It was over his shoulder, and indistinctly, that he first thought he saw a face; a little evil wedge-shaped face, looking out at him from a hole. When he turned and confronted it, the thing had vanished.

He quickened his pace, telling himself cheerfully not to begin imagining things, or there would be simply no end to it. He passed another hole, and another, and another; and then—yes!—no!—yes! certainly a little narrow face, with hard eyes, had flashed up for an instant from a hole, and was gone. He hesitated—braced himself up for an effort and strode on. Then suddenly, and as if it had been so all the time, every hole, far and near, and there were hundreds of them, seemed to possess its face, coming and going rapidly, all fixing on him glances of malice and hatred: all hard-eyed and evil and sharp.

If he could only get away from the holes in the banks, he thought, there would be no more faces. He swung off the path and plunged into the untrodden places of the wood.

Then the whistling began.

Very faint and shrill it was; and far behind him, when first he heard it; but somehow it made him hurry forward. Then, still very faint and shrill, it sounded far ahead of him, and made him hesitate and want to go back. As he halted in indecision it broke out on either side, and seemed to be caught up and passed on throughout the whole length of the wood to its farthest limit.

They were up and alert and ready, evidently, whoever they were! And he—he was alone, and unarmed, and far from any help; and the night was closing in.

Then the pattering began.

He thought it was only falling leaves at first, so slight and delicate was the sound of it. Then as it grew it took a regular rhythm, and he knew it for nothing else but the pat-pat-pat of little feet still a very long way off. Was it in front or behind? It seemed to be first one, and then the other, then both. It grew and it multiplied, till from every quarter as he listened anxiously, leaning this way and that, it seemed to be closing in on him. As he stood still to hearken, a rabbit came running hard towards him through the trees. He waited, expecting it to slacken pace, or to swerve from him into a different course. Instead, the animal almost brushed him as it dashed past, his face set and hard, his eyes staring. 'Get out of this, you fool, get out!' the Mole heard him mutter as he swung round a stump and disappeared down a friendly burrow.

The pattering increased till it sounded like sudden hail on the dry leaf-carpet spread around him. The whole wood seemed running now, running hard, hunting, chasing, closing in round something or—somebody? In panic, he began to run too, aimlessly, he knew not whither. He ran up against things, he fell over things and into things, he darted under things and dodged round things. At last he took refuge in the deep dark hollow of an old beech tree, which offered shelter, concealment—perhaps even safety, but who could tell? Anyhow, he was too tired to run any further, and could only snuggle down into the dry leaves which had drifted into the hollow and hope he was safe for a time. And as he lay there panting and trembling, and listened to the whistlings and the patterings outside, he knew it at last, in all its fullness, that dread thing which other little dwellers in field and hedgerow had encountered here, and known as their darkest moments—that thing which the Rat had vainly tried to shield him from—the Terror of the Wild Wood!

Meantime the Rat, warm and comfortable, dozed by his fireside. His paper and half-finished verses slipped from his knee, his head fell back, his mouth opened, and he wandered by the verdant banks of dream-rivers. Then a coal slipped, the fire crackled and sent up a spurt of flame, and he woke with a start. Remembering what he had been engaged upon, he reached down to the floor for his verses, pored over them for a minute, and then looked around for the Mole to ask him if he knew a good rhyme for something or other.

But the Mole was not there.

He listened for a time. The house seemed very quiet.

Then he called 'Moly!' several times, and, receiving no answer, got up and went into the hall.

The Mole's cap was missing from its accustomed peg. His goloshes, which always lay by the umbrella-stand, were also gone.

The Rat left the house, and carefully examined the muddy surface of the ground outside, hoping to find the mole's tracks. There they were, sure enough. The goloshes were new, just bought for the winter, and the pimples on their soles were fresh and sharp. He could see the imprints of them in the mud, running along straight and purposeful, leading direct to the Wild Wood.

The Rat looked very grave, and stood in deep thought for a minute or two. Then he re-entered the house, strapped a belt around his waist, shoved a brace of pistols into it, took up a stout cudgel that stood in a corner of the hall, and set off for the Wild Wood at a smart pace.

It was already getting towards dusk when he reached the first fringe of trees and plunged without hesitation into the wood, looking anxiously on either side for any sign of his friend. Here and there wicked little faces popped out of holes, but vanished immediately at sight of the valorous animal, his pistols, and the great ugly cudgel in his grasp; and the whistling and pattering, which he had heard quite plainly on his first entry, died away and ceased, and all was very still. He made his way manfully through the length of the wood, to its furthest edge; then, forsaking all paths, he set himself to traverse it, laboriously working over the whole ground, and all the time calling out cheerfully, 'Moly, Moly, Moly! Where are you? It's me–it's old Rat.'

He had patiently hunted through the wood for an hour or more, when at last to his joy he heard a little answering cry. Guiding himself by the sound, he made his way through the gathering darkness to the foot of an old beech tree, with a hole in it, and from out of the hole came a feeble voice, saying 'Ratty! Is that really you?'

The Rat crept into the hollow, and there he found the Mole, exhausted and still trembling. 'O Rat!' he cried, 'I've been so frightened, you can't think!'

'O, I quite understand,' said the Rat soothingly. 'You shouldn't really have gone and done it, Mole. I did my best to keep you from it. We river-bankers, we hardly ever come here by ourselves. If we have to come, we come in couples, at least; then we're generally all right. Besides, there are a hundred things one has to know, which we understand all about and you don't, as yet. I mean passwords, and signs, and sayings which have power and effect, and plants you carry in your pocket, and verses you repeat, and dodges and tricks you practise; all simple enough when you know them, but they've got to be known if you're small, or you'll find yourself in trouble. Of course if you were Badger or Otter, it would be quite another matter.'

'Surely the brave Mr. Toad wouldn't mind coming here by himself, would he?' inquired the Mole.

'Old Toad?' said the Rat, laughing heartily. 'He wouldn't show his face here alone, not for a whole hatful of golden guineas, Toad wouldn't.'

The Mole was greatly cheered by the sound of the Rat's careless laughter, as well as by the sight of his stick and his gleaming pistols, and he stopped shivering and began to feel bolder and more himself again.

'Now then,' said the Rat presently, 'we really must pull ourselves together and make a start for home while there's still a little light left. It will never do to spend the night here, you understand. Too cold, for one thing.'

'Dear Ratty,' said the poor Mole, 'I'm dreadfully sorry, but I'm simply dead beat and that's a solid fact. You *must* let me rest here a while longer, and get my strength back, if I'm to get home at all.'

'O, all right,' said the good-natured Rat, 'rest away. It's pretty nearly pitch dark now, anyhow; and there ought to be a bit of a moon later.'

So the Mole got well into the dry leaves and stretched himself out, and presently dropped off into sleep, though of a broken and troubled sort; while the Rat covered himself up, too, as best he might, for warmth, and lay patiently waiting, with a pistol in his paw.

When at last the Mole woke up, much refreshed and in his usual spirits, the Rat said, 'Now then! I'll just take a look outside and see if everything's quiet, and then we really must be off.'

He went to the entrance of their retreat and put his head out. Then the Mole heard him saying quietly to himself, 'Hullo! hullo! here–*is*–a–go!'

'What's up, Ratty?' asked the Mole.

'*Snow* is up,' replied the Rat briefly; 'or rather, *down*. It's snowing hard.'

The Mole came and crouched beside him, and, looking out, saw the wood that had been so dreadful to him in quite a changed aspect. Holes, hollows, pools, pitfalls, and other black menaces to the wayfarer were vanishing fast, and a gleaming carpet of faery was springing up everywhere, and that looked too delicate to be trodden upon by rough feet. A fine powder filled the air and caressed the cheek with a tingle in its touch, and the black boles of the trees showed up in a light that seemed to come from below.

'Well, well, it can't be helped,' said the Rat, after pondering. 'We must make a start, and take our chance, I suppose. The worst of it is, I don't exactly know where we are. And now this snow makes everything look so very different.'

It did indeed. The Mole would not have known that it was the same wood. However, they set out bravely, and took the line that seemed most promising, holding on to each other and pretending with invincible cheerfulness that they recognized an old friend in every fresh tree that grimly and silently greeted them, or saw openings, gaps, or paths with a familiar turn in them, in the monotony of white space and black tree-trunks that refused to vary.

An hour or so later–they had lost all count of time–they pulled up, dispirited, weary, and hopelessly at sea, and sat down on a fallen tree-trunk to recover their breath and consider what was to be done. They were aching with fatigue and bruised with tumbles; they had fallen into several holes and got wet through; the snow was getting so deep that they could hardly drag their little legs through it, and the trees were thicker and more like each other than ever. There seemed to be no end to this wood, and no beginning, and no difference in it, and, worst of all, no way out.

'We can't sit here very long,' said the Rat. 'We shall have to make another push for it, and do something or other. The cold is too awful for anything, and the snow will soon be too deep for us to wade through.' He peered about him and considered. 'Look here,' he went on, 'this is what occurs to me. There's a sort of dell down here in front of us, where the ground seems all hilly and bumpy and hummocky. We'll make our way down into that, and try and find some sort of shelter, a cave or hole with a dry floor to it, out of the snow and the wind, and there we'll have a good rest before we try again, for we're both of us pretty dead beat. Besides, the snow may leave off, or something may turn up.'

So once more they got on their feet, and struggled down into the dell, where they hunted about for a cave or some corner that was dry and a protection from the keen wind and the whirling snow. They were investigating one of the hummocky bits the Rat had spoken of, when suddenly the Mole tripped up and fell forward on his face with a squeal.

'O my leg!' he cried. 'O my poor shin!' and he sat up on the snow and nursed his leg in both his front paws.

'Poor old Mole!' said the Rat kindly. 'You don't seem to be having much luck to-day, do you? Let's have a look at the leg. Yes,' he went on, going down on his knees to look, 'you've cut your shin, sure enough. Wait till I get at my handkerchief, and I'll tie it up for you.'

'I must have tripped over a hidden branch or a stump,' said the Mole miserably. 'O, my! O, my!'

'It's a very clean cut,' said the Rat, examining it again attentively. 'That was never done by a branch or a stump. Looks as if it was made by a sharp edge of something in metal. Funny!' He pondered awhile, and examined the humps and slopes that surrounded them.

'Well, never mind what done it,' said the Mole, forgetting his grammar in his pain. 'It hurts just the same, whatever done it.'

But the Rat, after carefully tying up the leg with his handkerchief, had left him and was busy scraping in the snow. He scratched and shovelled and explored, all four legs working busily, while the Mole waited impatiently, remarking at intervals, 'O, *come* on, Rat!'

Suddenly the Rat cried 'Hooray!' and then 'Hoo-ray-oo-ray-oo-ray-oo-ray!' and fell to executing a feeble jig in the snow.

'What *have* you found, Ratty?' asked the Mole, still nursing his leg.

'Come and see!' said the delighted Rat, as he jigged on.

The Mole hobbled up to the spot and had a good look.

'Well,' he said at last, slowly, 'I *see* it right enough. Seen the same sort of thing before, lots of times. Familiar object, I call it. A door-scraper! Well, what of it? Why dance jigs around a door-scraper?'

'But don't you see what it *means*, you—you dull-witted animal?' cried the Rat impatiently.

'Of course I see what it means,' replied the Mole. 'It simply means that some *very* careless and forgetful person has left his door-scraper lying about in the middle of the Wild Wood, *just* where it's *sure* to trip *everybody* up. Very thoughtless of him, I call it. When I get home I shall go and complain about it to—to somebody or other, see if I don't!'

'O dear! O, dear!' cried the Rat, in despair at his obtuseness. 'Here, stop arguing and come and scrape!' And he set to work again and made the snow fly in all directions around him.

After some further toil his efforts were rewarded, and a very shabby door-mat lay exposed to view.

'There, what did I tell you?' exclaimed the Rat in great triumph.

'Absolutely nothing, whatever,' replied the Mole, with perfect truthfulness. 'Well now,' he went on, 'you seem to have found another piece of domestic litter, done for and thrown away, and

I suppose you're perfectly happy. Better go ahead and dance your jig round that if you've got to, and get it over, and then perhaps we can go on and not waste any more time over rubbish-heaps. Can we *eat* a door-mat? Or sleep under a door-mat? Or sit on a door-mat and sledge home over the snow on it, you exasperating rodent?'

'Do–you–mean–to–say,' cried the excited Rat, 'that this door-mat doesn't *tell* you anything?'

'Really, Rat,' said the Mole, quite pettishly, 'I think we'd had enough of this folly. Who ever heard of a door-mat *telling* any-one anything? They simply don't do it. They are not that sort at all. Door-mats know their place.'

'Now look here, you–you thick-headed beast,' replied the Rat, really angry, 'this must stop. Not another word, but scrape–scrape and scratch and dig and hunt round, especially on the sides of the hummocks, if you want to sleep dry and warm tonight, for it's our last chance!'

The Rat attacked a snow-bank beside them with ardour, probing with his cudgel everywhere and then digging with fury; and the Mole scraped busily too, more to oblige the Rat than for any other reason, for his opinion was that his friend was getting light-headed.

Some ten minutes' hard work, and the point of the Rat's cudgel struck something that sounded hollow. He worked till he could get a paw through and feel; then called the Mole to come and help him. Hard at it went the two animals, till at last the result of their labours stood full in view of the astonished and hitherto incredulous Mole.

In the side of what had seemed to be a snowbank stood a solid-looking little door, painted a dark green. An iron bell-pull hung by the side, and below it, on a small brass plate, neatly engraved in square capital letters, they could read by the aid of moonlight

MR. BADGER.

The Mole fell backwards on the snow from sheer surprise and delight. 'Rat!' he cried in penitence, 'you're a wonder! A real wonder, that's what you are. I see it all now! You argued it out, step by step, in that wise head of yours, from the very moment that I fell and cut my shin, and you looked at the cut, and at once your majestic mind said to itself, "Door-scraper!" And then you turned to and found the very door-scraper that done it! Did you stop there? No. Some people would have been quite satisfied; but not you. Your intellect went on working. "Let me only just find a door-mat," says you to yourself, "and my theory is proved!" And of course you found your door-mat. You're so clever, I believe you could find anything you liked. "Now," says you, "that door exists, as plain as if I saw it. There's nothing else remains to be done but to find it!" Well, I've read about that sort of thing in books, but I've never come across it before in real life. You ought to go where you'll be properly appreciated. You're simply wasted here, among us fellows. If I only had your head, Ratty——'

'But as you haven't,' interrupted the Rat, rather unkindly, 'I suppose you're going to sit on the snow all night and *talk*? Get up at once and hang on to that bell-pull you see there, and ring hard, as hard as you can, while I hammer!'

While the Rat attacked the door with his stick, the Mole sprang up at the bell-pull, clutched it and swung there, both feet well off the ground, and from quite a long way off they could faintly hear a deep-toned bell respond.

PROLOGUE from ANDROCLES and the LION

GEORGE BERNARD SHAW

George Bernard Shaw, not usually thought of as a writer of animal stories, is the author of one of the most famous, ANDROCLES AND THE LION *(1916). In this "comedy of saintliness," there is an amusing encounter between an injured lion and the kindly Christian who befriends him.*

[OVERTURE: *forest sounds, roaring of lions, Christian hymn faintly.*

A jungle path. A lion's roar, a melancholy suffering roar, comes from the jungle. It is repeated nearer. The lion limps from the jungle on three legs, holding up his right forepaw, in which a huge thorn sticks. He sits down and contemplates it. He licks it. He shakes it. He tries to extract it by scraping it along the ground, and hurts himself worse. He roars piteously. He licks it again. Tears drop from his eyes. He limps painfully off the path and lies down under the trees, exhausted with pain. Heaving a long sigh, like wind in a trombone, he goes to sleep.

Androcles and his wife Megaera come along the path. He is a small, thin, ridiculous little man who might be any age from thirty to fifty-five. He has sandy hair, watery compassionate blue eyes, sensitive nostrils, and a very presentable forehead; but his good points go no further: his arms and legs and back, though wiry of their kind, look shrivelled and starved. He carries a big bundle, is very poorly clad, and seems tired and hungry.

His wife is a rather handsome pampered slattern, well fed and in the prime of life. She has nothing to carry, and has a stout stick to help her along.]

MEGAERA [*suddenly throwing down her stick*]. I won't go another step.

ANDROCLES [*pleading wearily*]. Oh, not again, dear. What's the good of stopping every two miles and saying you won't go another step? We must get on to the next village before night. There are wild beasts in this wood: lions, they say.

MEGAERA. I don't believe a word of it. You are always threatening me with wild beasts to make me walk the very soul out of my body when I can hardly drag one foot before another. We haven't seen a single lion yet.

ANDROCLES. Well, dear, do you want to see one?

MEGAERA [*tearing the bundle from his back*]. You cruel brute, you don't care how tired I am, or what becomes of me [*she throws the bundle on the ground*]: always thinking of yourself. Self! self! self! always yourself! [*She sits down on the bundle.*]

ANDROCLES [*sitting down sadly on the ground with his elbows on his knees and his head in his hands*]. We all have to think of ourselves occasionally, dear.

MEGAERA. A man ought to think of his wife sometimes.

ANDROCLES. He can't always help it, dear. You make me think of you a good deal. Not that I blame you.

MEGAERA. Blame me! I should think not indeed. Is it my fault that I'm married to you?

ANDROCLES. No, dear: that is my fault.

MEGAERA. That's a nice thing to say to me. Aren't you happy with me?

ANDROCLES. I don't complain, my love.

MEGAERA. You ought to be ashamed of yourself.

ANDROCLES. I am, my dear.

MEGAERA. You're not: you glory in it.

ANDROCLES. In what, darling?

MEGAERA. In everything. In making me a slave, and making yourself a laughing-stock. It's not fair. You get me the name of being a shrew with your meek ways, always talking as if butter wouldn't melt in your mouth. And just because I look a big strong woman, and because I'm goodhearted and a bit hasty, and because you're always driving me to do things I'm sorry for afterwards, people say "Poor man: what a life his wife leads him!" Oh, if they only knew! And you think I don't know. But I do, I do, [*screaming*] I do.

ANDROCLES. Yes, my dear: I know you do.

MEGAERA. Then why don't you treat me properly and be a good husband to me?

ANDROCLES. What can I do, my dear?

MEGAERA. What can you do! You can return to your duty, and come back to your home and your friends, and sacrifice to the gods as all respectable people do, instead of having us hunted out of house and home for being dirty disreputable blaspheming atheists.

ANDROCLES. I'm not an atheist, dear: I am a Christian.

MEGAERA. Well, isn't that the same thing, only ten times worse? Everybody knows that the Christians are the very lowest of the low.

ANDROCLES. Just like us, dear.

MEGAERA. Speak for yourself. Don't you dare to compare me to common people. My father owned his own public-house; and sorrowful was the day for me when you first came drinking in our bar.

ANDROCLES. I confess I was addicted to it, dear. But I gave it up when I became a Christian.

MEGAERA. You'd much better have remained a drunkard. I can forgive a man being addicted to drink: it's only natural; and I don't deny I like a drop myself sometimes. What I can't stand is your being addicted to Christianity. And what's worse again, your being addicted to animals. How is any woman to keep her house clean when you bring in every stray cat and lost cur and lame duck in the whole countryside? You took the bread out of my mouth to feed them: you know you did: don't attempt to deny it.

ANDROCLES. Only when they were hungry and you were getting too stout, dearie.

MEGAERA. Yes: insult me, do. [*Rising*] Oh! I won't bear it another moment. You used to sit and talk to those dumb brute beasts for hours, when you hadn't a word for me.

ANDROCLES. They never answered back, darling. [*He rises and again shoulders the bundle.*]

MEGAERA. Well, if you're fonder of animals than of your own wife, you can live with them here in the jungle. I've had enough of them and enough of you. I'm going back. I'm going home.

ANDROCLES [*barring the way back*]. No, dearie: don't take on like that. We can't go back. We've sold everything: we should starve; and I should be sent to Rome and thrown to the lions—

MEGAERA. Serve you right! I wish the lions joy of you. [*Screaming*] Are you going to get out of my way and let me go home?

ANDROCLES. No, dear—

MEGAERA. Then I'll make my way through the forest; and when I'm eaten by the wild beasts you'll know what a wife you've lost. [*She dashes into the jungle and nearly falls over the sleeping lion.*] Oh! Oh! Andy! Andy! [*She totters back and collapses into the arms of Androcles, who, crushed by her weight, falls on his bundle.*]

ANDROCLES [*extracting himself from beneath her and slapping her hands in great anxiety*]. What is it, my precious, my pet? What's the matter? [*He raises her head. Speechless with terror, she points in the direction of the sleeping lion. He steals cautiously toward the spot indicated by Megaera. She rises with an effort and totters after him.*]

MEGAERA. No, Andy: you'll be killed. Come back.

[*The lion utters a long snoring sigh. Androcles sees the lion, and recoils fainting into the arms of Megaera, who falls back on the bundle. They roll apart and lie staring in terror at one another. The lion is heard groaning heavily in the jungle.*]

ANDROCLES [*whispering*]. Did you see? A lion.

MEGAERA [*despairing*]. The gods have sent him to punish us because you're a Christian. Take me away, Andy. Save me.

ANDROCLES [*rising*]. Meggy: there's one chance for you. It'll take him pretty nigh twenty minutes to eat me (I'm rather stringy and tough) and you can escape in less time than that.

MEGAERA. Oh, don't talk about eating. [*The lion rises with a great groan and limps towards them.*] Oh! [*She faints.*]

ANDROCLES [*quaking, but keeping between the lion and Megaera*]. Don't you come near my wife, do you hear? [*The lion groans. Androcles can hardly stand for trembling.*] Meggy: run. Run for your life. If I take my eye off him, it's all up. [*The lion holds up his wounded paw and flaps it piteously before Androcles.*] Oh, he's lame, poor old chap! He's got a thorn in his paw. A frightfully big thorn. [*Full of sympathy*] Oh, poor old man? Did um get an awful thorn into um's toosums wootsums? Has it made um too sick to eat a nice little Christian man for um's breakfast? Oh, a nice little Christian man will get um's thorn out for um; and then um shall eat the nice Christian man and the nice Christian man's nice big tender wifey pifey. [*The lion responds by moans of self-pity.*] Yes, yes, yes, yes, yes. Now, now [*taking the paw in his hand*], um is not to bite and not to scratch, not even if it hurts a very very little. Now make velvet paws. That's right. [*He pulls gingerly at the thorn. The lion, with an angry yell of pain, jerks back his paw so abruptly that Androcles is thrown on his back.*] Steadeee! Oh, did the nasty cruel little Christian man hurt the sore paw? [*The lion moans assentingly but apologetically.*] Well, one more little pull and it will be all over. Just one little, little, leetle pull; and then um will live happily ever after. [*He gives the thorn another pull. The lion roars and snaps his jaws with a terrifying clash.*] Oh, mustn't frighten um's good kind doctor, um's affectionate nursey. That didn't hurt at all: not a bit. Just one more. Just to shew how the brave big lion can bear pain, not like the little crybaby Christian man. Oopsh! [*The thorn comes out. The lion yells with pain, and shakes his paw wildly.*] That's it! [*Holding up the thorn.*] Now it's out. Now lick um's paw to take away the nasty inflammation. See? [*He licks his own hand. The lion nods intelligently and licks his paw industriously.*] Clever little liony-piony! Understands um's dear old friend Andy Wandy. [*The lion licks his face.*] Yes, kissums Andy Wandy. [*The lion, wagging his tail violently, rises on his hind legs, and embraces Androcles, who makes a wry face and cries.*] Velvet paws! Velvet paws! [*The lion draws in his claws.*] That's right. [*He embraces the lion, who finally takes the end of his tail in one paw, places that tight round Androcles' waist, resting it on his hip. Androcles takes the other paw in his hand, stretches out his arm, and the two waltz rapturously round and round and finally away through the jungle.*]

SILENCE—A FABLE

EDGAR ALLAN POE

—a selection from TALES OF MYSTERY AND IMAGINATION *(1839-42), by Edgar Allan Poe.*

Edgar Allan Poe was a master at portraying terror, and in this tale he evokes that emotion from one of the most frightening aspects of the wilderness—silence.

"Listen to me," said the demon, as he placed his hand upon my head. "The region of which I speak is a dreary region in Libya, by the borders of the river Zaïre, and there is no quiet there, nor silence.

"The waters of the river have a saffron and sickly hue; and they flow not onward to the sea, but palpitate forever and forever beneath the red eye of the sun with tumultuous and convulsive motion. For many miles on either side of the river's oozy bed is a pale desert of gigantic water-lilies. They sigh one unto the other in that solitude, and stretch toward the heavens their long and ghastly necks, and nod to and fro their everlasting heads. And there is an indistinct murmur which cometh out from among them like the rushing of subterrene water. And they sigh one unto the other.

"But there is a boundary to their realm—the boundary of the dark, horrible, lofty forest. There, like the waves about the Hebrides, the low underwood is agitated continually. But there is no wind throughout the heavens. And the tall primeval trees rock eternally hither and thither with a crashing and mighty sound. And from their high summits, one by one, drop everlasting dews. And at the roots strange poisonous flowers lie writhing in perturbed slumber. And overhead, with a rustling and loud noise, the gray clouds rush westwardly forever, until they roll, a cataract, over the fiery wall of the horizon. But there is no wind throughout the heaven. And by the shores of the river Zaïre there is neither quiet nor silence.

"It was night, and the rain fell; and, falling, it was rain, but, having fallen, it was blood. And I stood in the morass among the tall lilies, and the rain fell upon my head—and the lilies sighed one unto the other in the solemnity of their desolation.

"And, all at once, the moon arose through the thin ghastly mist, and was crimson in color. And mine eyes fell upon a huge gray rock which stood by the shore of the river, and was lighted by the light of the moon. And the rock was gray, and ghastly, and tall,—and the rock was gray. Upon its front were characters engraven in the stone; and I walked through the morass of water-lilies, until I came close unto the shore, that I might read the characters upon the stone. But I could not decipher them. And I was going back into the morass, when the moon shone with a fuller red, and I turned and looked again upon the rock, and upon the characters; and the characters were DESOLATION.

"And I looked upward, and there stood a man upon the summit of the rock; and I hid myself among the water-lilies that I might discover the actions of the man. And the man was tall and stately in form, and was wrapped up from his shoulders to his feet in the toga of old Rome. And the outlines of his figure were indistinct—but the features were the features of a deity; for the mantle of the night, and of the mist, and of the moon, and of the dew, had left uncovered the features of his face. And his brow was lofty with thought, and his eye wild with care; and in the few furrows upon his cheek I read the fables of sorrow, and weariness, and disgust with mankind, and a longing after solitude.

"And the man sat upon the rock, and leaned upon his hand, and looked out upon the desolation. He looked down into the low unquiet shrubbery, and up into the tall primeval trees, and up higher at the rustling heaven, and into the crimson moon. And I lay close within shelter of the lilies, and observed the actions of the man. And the man trembled in the solitude;—but the night waned, and he sat upon the rock.

"And the man turned his attention from the heaven, and looked out upon the dreary river Zaïre, and upon the yellow ghastly waters, and upon the pale legions of the water-lilies. And the man listened to the sighs of the water-lilies, and to the murmur that came up from among them. And I lay close within my covert and observed the actions of the man. And the man trembled in the solitude;—but the night waned and he sat upon the rock.

"Then I went down into the recesses of the morass and waded afar in among the wilderness of lilies, and called upon the hippopotami which dwelt among the fens in the recesses of the morass. And the hippopotami heard my call, and came, with the behemoth, unto the foot of the rock, and roared loudly and fearfully beneath the moon. And I lay close within my covert and observed the actions of the man. And the man trembled in solitude;—but the night waned and he sat upon the rock.

"Then I cursed the elements with the curse of tumult; and a frightful tempest gathered in the heaven, where, before, there had been no wind. And the heaven became livid with the violence of the tempest—and the rain beat upon the head of the man—and the floods of the river came down—and the river was tormented into foam—and the water-lilies shrieked within their beds—and the forest crumbled before the wind—and the thunder rolled—and the lightning fell—and the rock rocked to its foundation. And I lay close within my covert and observed the actions of the man. And the man trembled in the solitude;—but the night waned and he sat upon the rock.

"Then I grew angry and cursed, with the curse of *silence*, the river, and the lilies, and the wind, and the forest, and the heaven, and the thunder, and the sighs of the water-lilies. And they became accursed and *were still*. And the moon ceased to totter up its pathway to heaven—and the thunder died away—and the lightning did not flash—and the clouds hung motionless—and the waters sank to their level and remained—and the trees ceased to rock—and the water-lilies sighed no more—and the murmur was heard no longer from among them, nor any shadow of sound throughout the vast illimitable desert. And I looked upon the characters of the rock, and they were changed; and the characters were SILENCE.

"And mine eyes fell upon the countenance of the man, and his countenance was wan with terror. And, hurriedly, he raised his head from his hand, and stood forth upon the rock and listened. But there was no voice throughout the vast illimitable desert, and the characters upon the rock were SILENCE. And the man shuddered, and turned his face away, and fled afar off, in haste, so that I beheld him no more."

CHILDE ROLAND to the DARK TOWER CAME

ROBERT BROWNING

—one of Robert Browning's DRAMATIC ROMANCES *(1845).*
Man has often created his own landscapes of imagination.
These surrealistic scenes can be as vivid and compelling
in their effect upon the human emotions as any vistas
provided by nature. Such a landscape is depicted by
Robert Browning in his poem,
"Childe Roland to the Dark Tower Came."
Like most poems, it can be subjected
to various interpretations, but it seems plausible
to regard it as an allegory
of man's confrontation with the subconscious fears
of what Jung would call
the collective unconscious of the human race
transformed to a knightly quest
across a hideous wasteland.

(SEE EDGAR'S SONG IN "LEAR.")

I.

MY FIRST THOUGHT was, he lied in every word,
  That hoary cripple, with malicious eye
  Askance to watch the working of his lie
On mine, and mouth scarce able to afford
Suppression of the glee, that pursed and scored
  Its edge, at one more victim gained thereby.

II.

What else should he be set for, with his staff?
  What, save to waylay with his lies, ensnare
  All travellers who might find him posted there,
And ask the road? I guessed what skull-like laugh
Would break, what crutch 'gin write my epitaph
  For pastime in the dusty thoroughfare,

III.

If at his counsel I should turn aside
  Into that ominous tract which, all agree,
  Hides the Dark Tower. Yet acquiescingly
I did turn as he pointed: neither pride
Nor hope rekindling at the end descried,
  So much as gladness that some end might be.

IV.

For, what with my whole world-wide wandering,
  What with my search drawn out through years, my hope
  Dwindled into a ghost not fit to cope
With that obstreperous joy success would bring,—
I hardly tried now to rebuke the spring
  My heart made, finding failure in its scope.

V.

As when a sick man very near to death
  Seems dead indeed, and feels begin and end
  The tears, and takes the farewell of each friend,
And hears one bid the other go, draw breath
Freelier outside, ("since all is o'er," he saith,
  "And the blow fallen no grieving can amend;")

VI.

While some discuss if near the other graves
  Be room enough for this, and when a day
  Suits best for carrying the corpse away,
With care about the banners, scarves and staves:
And still the man hears all, and only craves
  He may not shame such tender love and stay.

VII.

Thus, I had so long suffered in this quest,
  Heard failure prophesied so oft, been writ
  So many times among "The Band"—to wit,
The knights who to the Dark Tower's search addressed
Their steps—that just to fail as they, seemed best,
  And all the doubt was now—should I be fit?

VIII.

So, quiet as despair, I turned from him,
  That hateful cripple, out of his highway
  Into the path he pointed. All the day
Had been a dreary one at best, and dim
Was settling to its close, yet shot one grim
  Red leer to see the plain catch its estray.

IX.

For mark! no sooner was I fairly found
  Pledged to the plain, after a pace or two,
  Than, pausing to throw backward a last view
O'er the safe road, 'twas gone; gray plain all round:
Nothing but plain to the horizon's bound.
  I might go on; nought else remained to do.

X.

So, on I went. I think I never saw
  Such starved ignoble nature; nothing throve:
  For flowers—as well expect a cedar grove!
But cockle, spurge, according to their law
Might propagate their kind, with none to awe,
  You'd think; a burr had been a treasure trove.

XI.

No! penury, inertness and grimace,
  In some strange sort, were the land's portion. "See
  Or shut your eyes," said Nature peevishly,
"It nothing skills: I cannot help my case:
'Tis the Last Judgment's fire must cure this place,
  Calcine its clods and set my prisoners free."

XII.

If there pushed any ragged thistle-stalk
  Above its mates, the head was chopped; the bents
  Were jealous else. What made those holes and rents
In the dock's harsh swarth leaves, bruised as to balk
All hope of greenness? 'tis a brute must walk
  Pashing their life out, with a brute's intents.

XIII.

As for the grass, it grew as scant as hair
  In leprosy; thin dry blades pricked the mud
  Which underneath looked kneaded up with blood.
One stiff blind horse, his every bone a-stare,
Stood stupefied, however he came there:
  Thrust out past service from the devil's stud!

XIV.

Alive? he might be dead for aught I know,
  With that red gaunt and colloped neck a-strain,
  And shut eyes underneath the rusty mane;
Seldom went such grotesqueness with such woe;
I never saw a brute I hated so;
  He must be wicked to deserve such pain.

XV.

I shut my eyes and turned them on my heart.
  As a man calls for wine before he fights,
  I asked one draught of earlier, happier sights,
Ere fitly I could hope to play my part.
Think first, fight afterwards—the soldier's art:
  One taste of the old time sets all to rights.

XVI.

Not it! I fancied Cuthbert's reddening face
  Beneath its garniture of curly gold,
  Dear fellow, till I almost felt him fold
An arm in mine to fix me to the place,
That way he used. Alas, one night's disgrace!
  Out went my heart's new fire and left it cold.

XVII.

Giles then, the soul of honor—there he stands
  Frank as ten years ago when knighted first.
  What honest man should dare (he said) he durst.
Good—but the scene shifts—faugh! what hangman hands
Pin to his breast a parchment? His own bands
  Read it. Poor traitor, spit upon and curst!

XVIII.

Better this present than a past like that;
  Back therefore to my darkening path again!
  No sound, no sight as far as eye could strain.
Will the night send a howlet or a bat?
I asked: when something on the dismal flat
  Came to arrest my thoughts and change their train.

XIX.

A sudden little river crossed my path
  As unexpected as a serpent comes.
  No sluggish tide congenial to the glooms;
This, as it frothed by, might have been a bath
For the fiend's glowing hoof—to see the wrath
  Of its black eddy bespate with flakes and spumes.

XX.

So petty yet so spiteful! All along,
  Low scrubby alders kneeled down over it;
  Drenched willows flung them headlong in a fit
Of mute despair, a suicidal throng:
The river which had done them all the wrong,
  Whate'er that was, rolled by, deterred no whit.

XXI.

Which, while I forded,–good saints, how I feared
  To set my foot upon a dead man's cheek,
  Each step, or feel the spear I thrust to seek
For hollows, tangled in his hair or beard!
–It may have been a water-rat I speared,
  But, ugh! it sounded like a baby's shriek.

XXII.

Glad was I when I reached the other bank.
  Now for a better country. Vain presage!
  Who were the strugglers, what war did they wage,
Whose savage trample thus could pad the dank
Soil to a plash? Toads in a poisoned tank,
  Or wild cats in a red-hot iron cage–

XXIII.

The fight must so have seemed in that fell cirque.
  What penned them there, with all the plain to choose?
  No footprint leading to that horrid mews,
None out of it. Mad brewage set to work
Their brains, no doubt, like galley-slaves the Turk
  Pits for his pastime, Christians against Jews.

XXIV.

And more than that–a furlong on–why, there!
  What bad use was that engine for, that wheel,
  Or brake, not wheel–that harrow fit to reel
Men's bodies out like silk? with all the air
Of Tophet's tool, on earth left unaware,
  Or brought to sharpen its rusty teeth of steel.

XXV.

Then came a bit of stubbed ground, once a wood,
  Next a marsh, it would seem, and now mere earth
  Desperate and done with; (so a fool finds mirth,
Makes a thing and then mars it, till his mood
Changes and off he goes!) within a rood–
  Bog, clay and rubble, sand and stark black dearth.

XXVI.

Now blotches rankling, colored gay and grim,
  Now patches where some leanness of the soil's
  Broke into moss or substances like boils;
Then came some palsied oak, a cleft in him
Like a distorted mouth that splits its rim
  Gaping at death, and dies while it recoils.

XXVII.

And just as far as ever from the end!
  Nought in the distance but the evening, nought
  To point my footstep further! At the thought,
A great black bird, Apollyon's bosom-friend,
Sailed past, nor beat his wide wing dragon-penned
  That brushed my cap—perchance the guide I sought.

XXVIII.

For, looking up, aware I somehow grew,
  'Spite of the dusk, the plain had given place
  All round to mountains—with such name to grace
Mere ugly heights and heaps now stolen in view.
How thus they had surprised me,—solve it, you!
  How to get from them was no clearer case.

XXIX.

Yet half I seemed to recognize some trick
  Of mischief happened to me, God knows when—
  In a bad dream perhaps. Here ended, then,
Progress this way. When, in the very nick
Of giving up, one time more, came a click
  As when a trap shuts—you're inside the den!

XXX.

Burningly it came on me all at once,
  This was the place! those two hills on the right,
  Crouched like two bulls locked horn in horn in fight;
While to the left, a tall scalped mountain . . . Dunce,
Dotard, a-dozing at the very nonce,
  After a life spent training for the sight!

XXXI.

What in the midst lay but the Tower itself?
  The round squat turret, blind as the fool's heart,
  Built of brown stone, without a counterpart
In the whole world. The tempest's mocking elf
Points to the shipman thus the unseen shelf
  He strikes on, only when the timbers start.

XXXII.

Not see? because of night perhaps?—why, day
  Came back again for that! before it left,
  The dying sunset kindled through a cleft:
The hills, like giants at a hunting, lay,
Chin upon hand, to see the game at bay,—
  "Now stab and end the creature—to the heft!"

XXXIII.

Not hear? when noise was everywhere! it tolled
  Increasing like a bell. Names in my ears,
  Of all the lost adventurers my peers,—
How such a one was strong, and such was bold,
And such was fortunate, yet each of old
  Lost, lost! one moment knelled the woe of years.

XXXIV.

There they stood, ranged along the hillsides, met
  To view the last of me, a living frame
  For one more picture! in a sheet of flame
I saw them and I knew them all. And yet
Dauntless the slug-horn to my lips I set,
  And blew. "*Childe Roland to the Dark Tower came.*"

PART III

Adventures into the Unknown

COLUMBUS and the VAGABOND BIRDS

MARY LEISTER

In the course of going about their own business, nature's creatures often cheer the hearts of men, without being at all aware that they are doing so. A notable example of this occurred during Columbus' first voyage to the New World. Land birds perched in the rigging of Columbus' ships gave his men the comforting assurance that terra firma *was at hand, and narrowly averted a mutiny. The suspense of this epic voyage is vividly recreated by Mary Leister in her article, "Columbus and the Vagabond Birds," which appeared in the October-November, 1965 issue of* NATIONAL WILDLIFE.

Christopher Columbus was a bird watcher. His terrified and rebellious crewmen, on that first voyage to the New World, were bird watchers, too. They may not, any of them, have known a hoopoe from a kite, but they knew that sea birds were sea birds and land birds were land birds and that one never ventured more than half a day's flight into the realm of the other. This was the unfounded article of faith that actually carried the reluctantly heroic expedition across the forlorn waters of the Atlantic.

The *Pinta*, *Nina*, and *Santa Maria* stood nine days out from the Canary Islands—nine days out on the Unknown Sea. For all those nine fear-wracked days there had been nothing but grey-green water beneath them and a grey-green sky overhead and a whistling green wind that hurtled them along, and soon it would all end. Soon—within the next hour, or the next minute—the three ships would sail out over the saucer rim of the world.

And then two birds, two *land* birds, flew across the *Nina*, incredibly headed into the vast emptiness beyond. The sailors cheered. Tomorrow or the day after would bring them safe to land.

But four days passed and no land came in sight. Even the most loyal crewmen performed their tasks laggardly, their minds filled with dragging fears. The westerly variations of the compass terrified the knowing seamen, and the Captain General kept a double reckoning—one for the eyes of his crew and a true one for himself.

Then a large flock of land birds flew over the ships and the *Pinta* broke the rules and raced off ahead of the company, following the birds to land. But they lost the birds, and there was no land, and the three little ships resumed their dismal wallowing in the grey-green sea.

On September 19th, a fearful fortnight out from the Canaries, two brown pelicans alighted on the *Santa Maria* and then "three little land birds perched in the rigging and sang merrily." Columbus, knowing a good bird when he saw one, made certain that every member of the crew of the *Santa Maria* saw those birds and that the news of their arrival was immediately given to the crews of the two companion caravels. For if *little* land birds could be so lightheartedly carefree out on the breast of the heaving deep, good solid earth could not be far away. The Indies and Cathay lay just beyond the horizon.

But each interminable day of sailing showed only the flatness of the unbroken sea. Provisions grew shorter, fresh water was vanishing, and the winds began to fall. Fear-filled grumblings rose in every dark and hidden corner of the three creeping ships. Sullen, mutinous men began to mutter that their Captain General should go overboard, and they quarrelled among themselves whether it should be by "accident" or by outright mutiny.

On September 25th the *Pinta* raised the cry of "Land!" But the sighted land was only a distant cloudbank, and hopelessness settled deeply upon the crews. Bitter, morose, on the edge of panic, the men were barely under control when a brown pelican swooped in for a landing on the yards and a flock of chittering sparrows settled briefly in the rigging. Those birds spelled l-a-n-d to the sea-weary sailors, and the sight of a pelican sleeping the afternoon away aboard their ship quieted them.

Day after day land birds came aboard the creaking ships, and day after day the sailors hailed their coming and strained red-rimmed eyes to search the horizon for the land that had to be but was not there.

On September 29th a frigate bird sailed the air currents above the lonely ships. The sailors gazed at him raptly for this bird, they *knew*, must return to land to sleep. He soared off on their compass heading and the three ships sailed on—and on—and on.

Day after endless day dropped by with nothing but empty skies and restless seas and falling winds—and little land birds flitting about in the rigging. Columbus' will was indomitable, his ambition keen, his authority over his men unwavering, but it was only the presence of those little land birds about his ships that tipped the scales of power in his favor and he knew it.

Then came a day, October third, when not a single bird was seen. Columbus was forced to use every power known to him to keep the seething mutiny from boiling over. In his own heart, now, there was fear—fear that they had passed by the islands he was certain were nearby.

The morning of October fourth showed them great flocks of tiny birds flying high overhead, flying steadily and continually toward the southwest. On October fifth, even greater flocks passed above them all day long. And all night the wakeful crew could hear a myriad of tiny calls as flock after flock flew over them.

Columbus did not know that those swift-flying birds were eskimo curlews and golden plovers on their unbelievable migratory flight from Labrador to South America, but he did know that they were birds with a purpose. He called his captains to a conference, and with their intense agreement, changed course to follow the birds. But at evening they had raised no land and an officer reported to Columbus, "Nothing seen today, Senor Captain, save some floating seagrass and some vagabond birds."

For four days they traveled to the southwest, following those vagabond birds. They sailed 280 leagues, but there was no land. The terrified sailors, bewildered by land birds that did not sleep but flew all night long over the endless sea, demanded that the ships turn back to Spain. But Columbus pointed to the unswerving flight of the great flocks above them and replied without a blink, "We are going to find the land we have come so far to seek."

On October 11th, with the endless flocks still flying overhead, the *Pinta* fished from the water a board and a stick that appeared to have been worked with iron, and the *Nina* sighted a branch covered with berries, "and with these signs all of them breathed and were glad."

At ten o'clock that night Columbus himself saw a light ahead and at two o'clock in the morning of October 12th, a sailor aboard the *Nina* hailed with a tremendous cheer the landfall ahead. Bathed in brilliant October moonlight, the New World rose out of the Unknown Sea, while above the rejoicing men great flocks of vagabond land birds still swept heedlessly along.

DE SOTO, LA SALLE, and the FATHER of WATERS

MARK TWAIN

—a selection from Life on the Mississippi *(1883), by Mark Twain.*

History need not be dull and tedious, as Samuel Clemens (better known as Mark Twain) demonstrates in his peppery commentary on the early explorers of the Mississippi. He is most entertaining as he speculates about why there was so little interest among explorers in the Mississippi from the time of its discovery by De Soto in 1542 to the late seventeenth century. Interspersed throughout Twain's account are some typically trenchant shafts of wit well aimed at the unconscious effrontery of European colonizers in converting the natives and expropriating their continent on behalf of a king across the water.

The date 1542, standing by itself, means little or nothing to us; but when one groups a few neighboring historical dates and facts around it, he adds perspective and color, and then realizes that this is one of the American dates which is quite respectable for age.

For instance, when the Mississippi was first seen by a white man, less than a quarter of a century had elapsed since Francis I.'s defeat at Pavia; the death of Raphael; the death of Bayard, *sans peur et sans reproche;* the driving out of the Knights-Hospitallers from Rhodes by the Turks; and the placarding of the Ninety-Five Propositions—the act which began the Reformation. When De Soto took his glimpse of the river, Ignatius Loyola was an obscure name; the order of the Jesuits was not yet a year old; Michelangelo's paint was not yet dry on the Last Judgment in the Sistine Chapel; Mary Queen of Scots was not yet born, but would be before the year closed. Catherine de Medici was a child; Elizabeth of England was not yet in her teens; Calvin,

Benvenuto Cellini, and the Emperor Charles V were at the top of their fame, and each was manufacturing history after his own peculiar fashion; Margaret of Navarre was writing the *Heptameron* and some religious books—the first survives, the others are forgotten, wit and indelicacy being sometimes better literature-preservers than holiness; lax court morals and the absurd chivalry business were in full feather, and the joust and the tournament were the frequent pastime of titled fine gentlemen who could fight better than they could spell, while religion was the passion of their ladies, and the classifying their offspring into children of full rank and children by brevet their pastime. In fact, all around, religion was in a peculiarly blooming condition: the Council of Trent was being called; the Spanish Inquisition was roasting, and racking, and burning with a free hand; elsewhere on the continent the nations were being persuaded to holy living by the sword and fire; in England, Henry VIII had suppressed the monasteries, burned Fisher and another bishop or two, and was getting his English reformation and his harem effectively started. When De Soto stood on the banks of the Mississippi, it was still two years before Luther's death; eleven years before the burning of Servetus; thirty years before the St. Bartholomew slaughter; Rabelais was not yet published; *Don Quixote* was not yet written; Shakespeare was not yet born; a hundred long years must still elapse before Englishmen would hear the name of Oliver Cromwell.

Unquestionably the discovery of the Mississippi is a datable fact which considerably mellows and modifies the shiny newness of our country, and gives her a most respectable outside-aspect of rustiness and antiquity.

De Soto merely glimpsed the river, then died and was buried in it by his priests and soldiers. One would expect the priests and the soldiers to multiply the river's dimensions by ten—the Spanish custom of the day—and thus move other adventurers to go at once and explore it. On the contrary, their narratives when they reached home did not excite that amount of curiosity. The Mississippi was left unvisited by whites during a term of years which seems incredible in our energetic days. One may "sense" the interval to his mind, after a fashion, by dividing it up in this way: After De Soto glimpsed the river, a fraction short of a quarter of a century elapsed, and then Shakespeare was born; lived a trifle more than half a century, then died; and when he had been in his grave considerably more than half a century, the *second* white man saw the Mississippi. In our day we don't allow a hundred and thirty years to elapse between glimpses of a marvel. If somebody should discover a creek in the county next to the one that the North Pole is in, Europe and America would start fifteen costly expeditions thither: one to explore the creek, and the other fourteen to hunt for each other.

For more than a hundred and fifty years there had been white settlements on our Atlantic coasts. These people were in intimate communication with the Indians: in the south the Spaniards were robbing, slaughtering, enslaving, and converting them; higher up, the English were trading beads and blankets to them for a consideration, and throwing in civilization and whisky, "for lagniappe";[1] and in Canada the French were schooling them in a rudimentary way, missionarying among them, and drawing whole populations of them at a time to Quebec, and later to Montreal, to buy furs of them. Necessarily, then, these various clusters of whites must have heard of the great river of the far west; and indeed, they did hear of it vaguely—so vaguely and indefinitely that its course, proportions, and locality were hardly even guessable. The mere mysteriousness of the matter ought to have fired curiosity and compelled exploration; but this did not occur. Apparently nobody happened to want such a river, nobody needed it, nobody was curious about it; so, for a century and a half the Mississippi remained out of the market and undisturbed. When De Soto found it, he was not hunting for a river, and had no present occasion for one; consequently he did not value it or even take any particular notice of it.

But at last La Salle the Frenchman conceived the idea of seeking out that river and exploring it. It always happens that when a man seizes upon a neglected and important idea, people inflamed with the same notion crop up all around. It happened so in this instance.

Naturally the question suggests itself, Why did these people want the river now when nobody had wanted it in the five preceding generations? Apparently it was because at this late day they thought they had discovered a way to make it useful; for it had come to be believed that the Mississippi emptied into the

---

[1] Something extra.

Gulf of California, and therefore afforded a short cut from Canada to China. Previously the supposition had been that it emptied into the Atlantic, or Sea of Virginia.

La Salle himself sued for certain high privileges, and they were graciously accorded him by Louis XIV of inflated memory. Chief among them was the privilege to explore, far and wide, and build forts, and stake out continents, and hand the same over to the king, and pay the expenses himself; receiving, in return, some little advantages of one sort or another; among them the monopoly of buffalo hides. He spent several years and about all of his money in making perilous and painful trips between Montreal and a fort which he had built on the Illinois, before he at last succeeded in getting his expedition in such a shape that he could strike for the Mississippi.

And meantime other parties had had better fortune. In 1673 Joliet the merchant, and Marquette the priest, crossed the country and reached the banks of the Mississippi. They went by way of the Great Lakes; and from Green Bay, in canoes, by way of Fox River and the Wisconsin. Marquette had solemnly contracted, on the feast of the Immaculate Conception, that if the Virgin would permit him to discover the great river, he would name it Conception, in her honor. He kept his word. In that day, all explorers traveled with an outfit of priests. De Soto had twenty-four with him. La Salle had several, also. The expeditions were often out of meat, and scant of clothes, but they always had the furniture and other requisites for the mass; they were always prepared, as one of the quaint chroniclers of the time phrased it, to "explain hell to the salvages."

On the 17th of June, 1673, the canoes of Joliet and Marquette and their five subordinates reached the junction of the Wisconsin with the Mississippi. Mr. Parkman says: "Before them a wide and rapid current coursed athwart their way, by the foot of lofty heights wrapped thick in forests." He continues: "Turning southward, they paddled down the stream, through a solitude unrelieved by the faintest trace of man."

A big catfish collided with Marquette's canoe, and startled him; and reasonably enough, for he had been warned by the Indians that he was on a foolhardy journey, and even a fatal one, for the river contained a demon "whose roar could be heard at a great distance, and who would engulf them in the abyss where he dwelt." I have seen a Mississippi catfish that was more than six feet long and weighed two hundred and fifty pounds; and if Marquette's fish was the fellow to that one, he had a fair right to think the river's roaring demon was come.

"At length the buffalo began to appear, grazing in herds on the great prairies which then bordered the river; and Marquette describes the fierce and stupid look of the old bulls as they stared at the intruders through the tangled mane which nearly blinded them."

The voyagers moved cautiously: "Landed at night and made a fire to cook their evening meal; then extinguished it, embarked again, paddled some way farther, and anchored in the stream, keeping a man on the watch till morning."

They did this day after day and night after night; and at the end of two weeks they had not seen a human being. The river was an awful solitude, then. And it is now, over most of its stretch.

But at the close of the fortnight they one day came upon the footprints of men in the mud of the western bank—a Robinson Crusoe experience which carries an electric shiver with it yet, when one stumbles on it in print. They had been warned that the river Indians were as ferocious and pitiless as the river demon, and destroyed all comers without waiting for provocation; but no matter, Joliet and Marquette struck into the country to hunt up the proprietors of the tracks. They found them, by and by, and were hospitably received and well treated—if to be received by an Indian chief who has taken off his last rag in order to appear at his level best is to be received hospitably; and if to be treated abundantly to fish, porridge, and other game, including dog, and have these things forked into one's mouth by the ungloved fingers of Indians is to be well treated. In the morning the chief and six hundred of his tribesmen escorted the Frenchmen to the river and bade them a friendly farewell.

On the rocks above the present city of Alton they found some rude and fantastic Indian paintings, which they describe. A short distance below "a torrent of yellow mud rushed furiously athwart the calm blue current of the Mississippi, boiling and surging and sweeping in its course logs, branches, and uprooted trees." This was the mouth of the Missouri, "that savage river," which "descending from its mad career through a vast unknown of barbarism, poured its turbid floods into the bosom of its gentle sister."

By and by they passed the mouth of the Ohio; they passed canebrakes; they fought mosquitoes; they floated along, day after day, through the deep silence and loneliness of the river, drowsing in the scant shade of makeshift awnings, and broiling with the heat; they encountered and exchanged civilities with another party of Indians; and at last they reached the mouth of the Arkansas (about a month out from their starting point), where a tribe of war-whooping savages swarmed out to meet and murder them; but they appealed to the Virgin for help; so in place of a fight there was a feast, and plenty of pleasant palaver and folderol.

They had proved to their satisfaction that the Mississippi did not empty into the Gulf of California, or into the Atlantic. They believed it emptied into the Gulf of Mexico. They turned back, now, and carried their great news to Canada.

But belief is not proof. It was reserved for La Salle to furnish the proof. He was provokingly delayed, by one misfortune after another, but at last got his expedition under way at the end of the year 1681. In the dead of winter he and Henri de Tonty, son of Lorenzo Tonty, who invented the tontine, his lieutenant, started down the Illinois, with a following of eighteen Indians brought from New England, and twenty-three Frenchmen. They moved in procession down the surface of the frozen river, on foot, and dragging their canoes after them on sledges.

At Peoria Lake they struck open water, and paddled thence to the Mississippi and turned their prows southward. They plowed through the fields of floating ice, past the mouth of the Missouri; past the mouth of the Ohio, by and by; "and, gliding by the wastes of bordering swamp, landed on the 24th of February near the Third Chickasaw Bluffs," where they halted and built Fort Prudhomme.

"Again," says Mr. Parkman, "they embarked; and with every stage of their adventurous progress, the mystery of this vast new world was more and more unveiled. More and more they entered the realms of spring. The hazy sunlight, the warm and drowsy air, the tender foliage, the opening flowers, betokened the reviving life of nature."

Day by day they floated down the great bends, in the shadow of the dense forests, and in time arrived at the mouth of the

Arkansas. First, they were greeted by the natives of this locality as Marquette had before been greeted by them—with the booming of the war drum and the flourish of arms. The Virgin composed the difficulty in Marquette's case; the pipe of peace did the same office for La Salle. The white man and the red man struck hands and entertained each other during three days. Then, to the admiration of the savages, La Salle set up a cross with the arms of France on it, and took possession of the whole country for the king—the cool fashion of the time—while the priest piously consecrated the robbery with a hymn. The priest explained the mysteries of the faith "by signs," for the saving of the savages; thus compensating them with possible possessions in Heaven for the certain ones on earth which they had just been robbed of. And also, by signs, La Salle drew from these simple children of the forest acknowledgments of fealty to Louis the Putrid, over the water. Nobody smiled at these colossal ironies.

These performances took place on the site of the future town of Napoleon, Arkansas, and there the first confiscation cross was raised on the banks of the great river. Marquette's and Joliet's voyage of discovery ended at the same spot—the site of the future town of Napoleon. When De Soto took his fleeting glimpse of the river, away back in the dim early days, he took it from that same spot—the site of the future town of Napoleon, Arkansas. Therefore, three out of the four memorable events connected with the discovery and exploration of the mighty river occurred, by accident, in one and the same place. It is a most curious distinction, when one comes to look at it and think about it. France stole that vast country on that spot, the future Napoleon; and by and by Napoleon himself was to give the country back again! —make restitution, not to the owners, but to their white American heirs.

The voyagers journeyed on, touching here and there; "passed the sites, since become historic, of Vicksburg and Grand Gulf"; and visited an imposing Indian monarch in the Teche country, whose capital city was a substantial one of sun-baked bricks mixed with straw—better houses than many that exist there now. The chief's house contained an audience room forty feet square; and there he received Tonty in State, surrounded by sixty old men clothed in white cloaks. There was a temple in the town, with a mud wall about it ornamented with skulls of enemies sacrificed to the sun.

The voyagers visited the Natchez Indians, near the site of the present city of that name, where they found a "religious and political despotism, a privileged class descended from the sun, a temple and a sacred fire." It must have been like getting home again; it was home with an advantage, in fact, for it lacked Louis XIV.

A few more days swept swiftly by, and La Salle stood in the shadow of his confiscating cross, at the meeting of the waters from Delaware, and from Itaska, and from the mountain ranges close upon the Pacific, with the waters of the Gulf of Mexico, his task finished, his prodigy achieved.

THE LEWIS and CLARK EXPEDITION

REUBEN GOLD THWAITES

—a selection from EARLY WESTERN TRAVELS *by Reuben Gold Thwaites, D. Appleton Co., 1904.*

When President Thomas Jefferson wanted someone to make an exploratory expedition into the West for a route to the Pacific, he chose his secretary, Captain Meriwether Lewis, to head it. Lewis then selected William Clark as his associate in command. Reuben Gold Thwaites' account of the expedition is drawn from the official journals kept by its leaders.

This excerpt begins as the expedition is proceeding up the Missouri River in late May, 1804 from what is now St. Charles, Missouri and what was then a French hamlet with a population of only about 450.

Difficulties commenced immediately. Violent currents swept around the great sandbars, in which the boats were often dangerously near swamping. Snags were numerous, and against these sprawling obstructions they were frequently hurled violently by the swirling waters; several times masts were broken by being caught in the branches. Now and then war-trails were seen, and a close watch was deemed essential to avoid possible surprise by bands of prowling savages, jealous of this formidable invasion of their hunting-grounds. Farther up the river—by the third week of September—high shelving banks, now and then undermined by the current and falling into the river in masses often many acres in extent, gave them great alarm; and not infrequently their craft, swept by the current to the foot of such an overhanging bluff of sand and clay, were in serious danger. [1]

---

[1] In a letter to his mother, dated Fort Mandan, March 31, 1805, Lewis states: "So far we have experienced more difficulties from the navigation

Rapids were now [mid-June, 1804] frequently met with, necessitating the use in the swift water of towing-lines and kedge-anchors, a work much impeded by heavy growths, along the banks, of bushes and gigantic weeds. "Ticks and musquiters," and great swarms of "knats," begin to be "verry troublesome," necessitating smudge fires and mosquito-bars. The men frequently suffer from snake-bites, sun-stroke, and stomach complaints. Both Lewis and Clark now play the part of physicians, and administer simple though sometimes drastic remedies for these disorders; the journals make frequent mention of strange doses and vigorous bleeding. Sometimes storms drench them in their rude camp; or suddenly bursting upon their craft in open river, necessitate great ado with anchors and cables until the flurry is over—as once, "when the Storm Sudenly Seased and the river became Instancetainously as Smoth as Glass."

[By the end of August, 1804, the expedition had passed the mouth of the Platte River and the present sites of Omaha, Nebraska and Sioux City, Iowa and had reached what is now Knox County in Nebraska.]

The explorers were now in a paradise of game. Great herds of buffaloes, sometimes five thousand strong, were grazing in the plains, the fattest of them falling easy victims to the excellent

---

of the Missouri than danger from the savages. The difficulties which oppose themselves to the navigation of this immense river arise from the rapidity of its current, its falling banks, sand-bars and timber which remains wholly or partially concealed in its bed, usually called by the navigators of the Missouri and the Mississippi 'sawyer' or 'planter'

"one of these difficulties the navigator never ceases to contend with from the Entrance of the Missouri to this place; and in innumerable instances most of these obstructions are at the same instant combined to oppose his progress or threaten his destruction. To these we may also add a fifth, and not much less considerable difficulty—the turbed quality of the water—which renders it impracticable to discover any obstruction, even to the depth of a single inch. Such is the velocity of the current at all seasons of the year, from the entrance of the Missouri to the mouth of the great river Platte, that it is impossible to resist its force by means of oars or poles in the main channel of the river; the eddies which therefore generally exist on one side or the other of the river, are sought by the navigators, but these are almost universally encumbered with concealed timber, or within reach of the falling banks."

aim of the hunters. Elk, deer, antelopes, turkeys, and squirrels were abundant, and gave variety to their meals, for which the navigators generally tied up at the bank and joined the land party around huge camp-fires. Prairie-dogs, whose little burrows punctured the plains in every direction, interested the explorers. One day there was a general attempt to drown out one of these nimble miners; but although all joined for some time in freely pouring water down the hole, the task was finally abandoned as impracticable. Prairie-wolves nightly howled about their camps in surprising numbers and in several varieties.

Worn by the fatigue of a day's hard work at the oars or the towing-line or pushing-pole, or perhaps by long hours of tramping or hunting upon the rolling plains, which were frequently furrowed by deep ravines, each member of the party earned his night's rest. But as they lay under the stars, around the generous fires of driftwood, great clouds of mosquitoes not infrequently robbed them of sleep. The two leaders were possessed of mosquito-bars, which generally enabled them to rest with comparative comfort, although sometimes even these were ineffectual; but apparently none of the others enjoyed these luxuries, and buried their heads within their blankets, almost to the point of suffocation. Once they had camped upon a sand-bar, in mid-river. By the light of the moon the guard saw the banks caving in above and below. Alarming the sleepers, they had barely time to launch and board their boats before the very spot where they had lain slipped into the turbid current. In the upper reaches of the river, the following year, grizzly bears and stampeded buffalo herds were added to the list of night terrors.

It was not always possible for the land and water parties to make connections for the night camps. The hunters and walkers were often obliged to take long detours into the interior, either in search of game or because of deep ravines or of steep bluffs bordering upon the river; and sometimes a cut-short was taken, to avoid the frequent bends of the winding stream. The heavy growth of timber and bushes along the banks often rendered it impossible for the land party to trace or even to see the water. The result was, that not infrequently the pedestrians and horsemen would lose sight of the boatsmen, and then it was impossible to say whether the former were above or below the latter. In the last week of August, one of the men, George Shannon, having the horses in charge—there were now several of them in the little herd—lost touch with his fellows and thought them ahead of him. For sixteen days he hurried on, without bullets to shoot game, and not only lost all his horses but one, but when finally caught up with by his comrades was in a starving condition. . . . even the leaders were sometimes lost in this manner and obliged to camp out alone in the wilderness, uncertain whether to hurry or to tarry.

[After spending the winter of 1804-05 in a log fort which they built near the villages of the Mandan Indians, located in the vicinity of the present Bismarck, North Dakota, the expedition started up the Missouri River again in early April and reached the mouth of the Yellowstone on the twenty-sixth of that month.]

In these upper regions, where signs of coal were frequently seen and in places alkali whitened the ground like snow, "game is very abundant and gentle"; two hunters could, Lewis thinks, "conveniently supply a regiment with provisions." Big-horns, monster elk, black and grizzly bears, antelopes, and great herds of buffaloes are daily met; they feast off beavers, Lewis thinking "the tale a most delicious morsel," and wondering greatly at the industry of these animals, which in some spots fell for their numerous dams many acres of timber as thick as a man's body; wolves increase, and the nimble coyotes begin to interest them.

The huge and savage grizzly was, in some respects, the most formidable obstacle encountered by the intrepid explorers; compared with these bulky, ferocious beasts, Indians occasioned small alarm. By the time the party were a month out from the Mandans, Lewis could write: "I find that the curiossity of our party is pretty well satisfyed with rispect to this anamal . . . [he] has staggered the resolution of several [of] them." A few days later came a disagreeable experience with a grizzly, in which he and seven of his men, as yet unable to locate the vulnerable parts, found it impossible to kill the creature save after a persistent fusillade from their short-range rifles. "These bear," he says, "being so hard to die reather intimeadates us all; I must confess that I do not like the gentlemen and had reather fight two Indians than one bear."

Both Lewis and Clark were fond of hunting, and one or the

other of them, more often Lewis, generally accompanied the hunters on shore; although, as in the lower reaches, the captain often wandered far from his party, collecting specimens or ascending elevations to examine the country. Lewis, when walking, was always armed both with his rifle and a halberd (or spontoon), which later he found convenient as a weapon and as a staff. One day he fell upon the edge of a bluff whose surface had been rendered slippery through rain; but a dexterous use of the halberd saved him from a fall of ninety feet, that no doubt would have been fatal.

At another time he had just shot a fat buffalo and, his rifle as yet unloaded, was watching the animal die, when he was startled to find that a large grizzly had stealthily crept within twenty paces of him. There were no bushes within several miles, the nearest tree was three hundred yards away, and the riverbank, eighty yards distant, sloped down to a height of not over three feet. At first he slowly retreated toward the tree, but the bear rushed at him with open mouth, at full speed. By turning on his track, the captain was able to reach the water, into which he ran until waist deep. Flourishing the halberd at the animal, the latter paused upon the shore, twenty paces distant, and suddenly showing alarm at this threatened attack, wheeled and ran away as fast as he could to the nearest woods.

But the enemy was not always thus easily frightened. On one occasion, an immense fellow so closely pursued two hunters who had poured eight bullets into his body that in their hasty retreat they cast aside their guns and pouches, and threw themselves into the river, over a perpendicular bank twenty feet high. The infuriated bear plunged in after them, only a few feet behind the second man, when fortunately another hunter on the shore shot the fellow through the head and killed him. Such sport lent zest to the journey, but soon gave rise to an order that the men must, when in open country, act only on the defensive with this ferocious creature.

Once, at the dead of night, a large buffalo bull invaded their camp. Apparently attracted by the light, he swam the river, and climbing over their best pirogue—but fortunately not seriously injuring it—he charged the fires at full speed, passing within a few inches of the heads of the sleeping men, and made for Lewis and Clark's tent. Lewis's dog, his constant companion throughout the expedition, caused the burly beast to change his course, and he was off in a flash; all this, before the sentinel could arouse the camp, which was now in an uproar, the men rushing out with guns in hand, inquiring for the cause of the disturbance.

Owing to the mismanagement of the steersman, a squall of wind caused the pirogue to upset. Papers, instruments, books, medicines, ammunition, and articles of merchandise were wet and nearly lost—a narrow escape from a disaster which might well have meant the end of the expedition. A camp-fire once crept into a tree overhanging the captains' lodge. The guard awakened them, and they removed the tent just in time to escape being crushed by the falling trunk. It would be easy to fill pages with experiences of this sort—with bears, buffaloes, wolves, tiger cats, and rattlesnakes, and with the forces of inanimate nature—which daily and nightly beset these hardy adventurers who, first of all white men, were breaking a transcontinental path westward to the Pacific.

ALASKAN GOLD RUSH

CARL J. LOMEN

Many a greenhorn prospector trying his luck in the Alaskan gold rush of 1900 found more adventure than he did gold. Such was the experience of Carl J. Lomen, who went to Nome in 1900, at the age of nineteen. He was joined by his lawyer father, and soon the entire Lomen family had moved from Minnesota to Alaska, not to pan for gold, but to develop a vast reindeer industry. However, Carl often recalled with nostalgia the fantastic gold rush days, vividly recorded in his book, Fifty Years in Alaska, *New York: David McKay Co., Inc., 1954.*

The first discovery of gold near Nome was in the fall of 1898. Only a few people managed to reach the scene of the strike before winter set in. A thousand more poured in when the 1899 season for prospecting opened up. Now, in 1900, came the big rush. Forty thousand people arrived from all parts of the world. The beach on which they landed bordered a timberless tundra. The word "tundra" had always intrigued me, suggesting something foreign, a touch of the Russian, perhaps. Now I learned at firsthand what it was really like: vast, treeless, largely level plains, with a mucky topsoil, and permanently frozen subsoil, supporting a dense growth of mosses and lichens, grasses, dwarf shrubs, willows and alder, and many varieties of flowers. Beyond "city limits" tundra characterizes the arctic regions in both hemispheres.

As a youngster of nineteen I was having the time of my life. I was too green to recognize a prospect if I fell over one, but I considered myself a prospector, nevertheless. Most of the men who came to Nome in 1900 were in the same category. In time we picked up the rudiments of prospecting for gold from the sourdoughs who had trekked down the Yukon River.

Those who went North during this period were, in the main, brave men. Most of them were poor, too, or they would not have struggled against the privation and danger. They worked killingly at a thankless task, never faltering, yet often failing. Some laid down their lives along the bleak shores of Bering Strait, overcome by cold winds and driving snows, scurvy and other diseases of a primitive environment.

United States federal laws stipulated that a sixty-foot strip of land along the Nome beach could not be subject to location. Miners, therefore, were limited to the area covered by a tent or tents, and the space under actual occupancy.

I had my fling at mining on the beach. Teaming up with a fine fellow named Alex Allen, I traveled some thirty miles west of Nome. Alex had been assistant physical director of the YMCA at Rochester, New York, and was no more of a miner than I.

We had a small wooden contraption, called a "rocker," some three and a half feet high, with a hopper on top and two burlap-covered frames leading down from it. On the lower section of the rocker there was a copper plate on which quick-silver was spread to amalgamate any fine gold that might wash down over it. Using a copper plate, we were forced to clean it every day with a solution of cyanide of potassium. A silver plate made daily cleaning unnecessary, but it was unobtainable at Nome. Some beach miners went to the trouble of lining their lower plate with silver dollars.

The square wooden frame of the hopper was open at the top, with a thin sheet of iron on the bottom, perforated like a sieve with holes about a quarter inch in diameter. A gallon tin can affixed to a heavy stick was used as a dipper.

Two men usually worked together, taking turns at the rocker. First you dropped a shovelful of sand or gravel into the hopper, then you dipped water over it until all the fine material was washed down, meanwhile rocking the equipment back and forth by means of a wooden handle fastened to the side. At intervals you removed the hopper to empty the coarser material, and repeated the process endlessly. While one of us operated the rocker, the other brought up the best pay dirt to be found in the vicinity. Any gold collecting on the burlap was washed off into a pan. Then the amalgam on the plate was burned off to evaporate the quicksilver. This was known as "retorted gold."

I think that one of history's strangest sights was that witnessed by the equally startled Eskimo and reindeer of the Bering Strait area as multitudes of white men and a few adventurous women, bitten by the goldbug, ranged up and down many miles of the beaches on both sides of Nome, ripping up the tundra in a frantic search for wealth beyond their dreams.

With the onslaught of the first storm of the season the beach miners had to give up their digging while the seas swept the shores clean. As soon as the storm had passed, the miners rushed back to the beach, but they were seldom able to find the holdings they had been working. Several storms so mixed up the sand that beach mining became profitless; and the prospectors packed their equipment and moved elsewhere. Yet in the summer of 1900 some $2,000,000 in gold was snatched from the beach sands; and a few of the more experienced miners took in upward of $1,000 a day with their rockers.

One stormy night our diggings were washed out by the sea and, after trying several other locations, Alex and I concluded that we were too far west for "pay dirt," and we returned to Nome.

A macabre note was to be found in connection with the graveyard that had been staked out at the western edge of Nome, where the dead were buried in shallow graves dug in the perpetually frozen earth. When it was discovered that Mother Nature had provided golden shrouds for the bodies buried there, the very graves were tunneled out with little respect given to the corpses.

Miners pursued "pay dirt" up and down the streets of Nome, ripping them up as they went along, sometimes even tearing down buildings that were under construction. Here at last in America was found a city whose streets were literally paved with gold!

Now I was a prospector, right enough, though I hadn't found enough gold to rate a notice on the back page of my home-town newspaper. Out into the hills I would go, sometimes alone, with my pack on my back, no tent, but with a primus stove, tarpaulin, and blanket. We miners usually worked all night, but it was no hardship as it was light around the clock. We slept during the warmth of the day. Everything was new and strange to me and, like any nineteen-year-old, I enjoyed it to the fullest.

One day, approaching a small pond, I saw my first swan. This beautiful creature, whiter than milk, paddled busily to outdistance me, breasting the water, carrying its graceful neck nobly. It sped to the opposite bank and, awkwardly flopping ashore, paused there to regard me. As I went on, it proudly took to the water again.

I made the discovery that the back country formed into fantastic shapes, like forts and battlements in a mythical kingdom. Here was a vast and lonesome land, big, barren, and yet majestic. It played tricks with a man's mind, tightening the belly and the heart.

I also found out about sub-Arctic insects, "nosee-ums" or mosquitoes, and black gnats. Insects swarmed out of the tundra moss in streams that ran like wisps of smoke, growing into circles that wheeled around a man's head. It did no good to fight them. Destroy a hundred and a thousand mobilized to take their place. They were not so bad along the ocean beaches; but inland, especially where there was no wind, they were a continual torment.

On these prospecting trips I had my first sample of the Arctic wind. A cold bully of a wind, strangely enough it drove not from the polar regions but from the coast and Siberia. It would let up for a moment, then come on again stronger than before. Lancing through stout clothing as though it were cheesecloth, it raised goose pimples on the skin, even when the sun shone brightly. The north wind blew across Seward Peninsula incessantly, though during the short summer season it was usually mild.

Shortly after we were established in our two-tent home on Belmont Point, Nome, Dad secured options on two placer mining claims some dozen or so miles away, on tributaries of the Snake River. We arranged for two men, whom we had met on the Garonne, to join me on a trip to prospect the claims.

We assembled our equipment: picks, shovels, blankets, gold pans, food, and cooking utensils. When all was ready, we struck out across the tundra, each with a fifty-pound pack strapped to his shoulders. Dad accompanied us for a couple of miles and then turned back to our home and the lawbook he was studying: the new civil and criminal code of Alaska, adopted by Congress the preceding winter. During our first year in Alaska, Dad checked that book from cover to cover.

We established our first camp, without tent or tarpaulins, on Balto Creek, where we spent several days digging shafts and panning the gravel for gold. We found some but not enough to call it "pay." The Balto was a very small creek with all wash gravel. There were some trout in the stream, which we caught and ate. The mosquitoes were so thick that we got very little sleep.

I was careful in my panning and saved the colors found, wrapping each prospect in a piece of paper. One evening we were visited by two miners who had been in the Klondike.

"How you making out, boys?" they asked.

"Oh, so-so," I said, producing our slim prospects.

"Want to see some real gold?" one of them offered.

"We sure do," I declared.

He dug into a hip pocket and took out a heavy poke. Opening it, he poured the contents into one of our pans. We stared at the nuggets ranging in value from a few dollars to around fifty dollars each.

"That's Klondike gold," I guessed.

"Right enough."

"Gosh," I exclaimed. "I hope I make a strike like that someday."

I'm still hoping.

VOYAGE to the SOUTH POLE

ROALD AMUNDSEN

By the dawn of the twentieth century, there was little unexplored wilderness left to challenge the adventurer except the North and South poles. The first man to reach the South Pole was the Norwegian explorer, Roald Amundsen, on December 14, 1911, less than a month before the Englishman, Robert Falcon Scott, arrived at the same destination, never to return. The following account of the culmination of Amundsen's travels in Antarctica is the explorer's own, taken from his book, The South Pole, *New York: L. Keedick, 1913.*

In Lat. 87° S.—according to dead reckoning—we saw the last of the land to the northeast. The atmosphere was then apparently as clear as could be, and we felt certain that our view covered all the land there was to be seen from that spot. We were deceived again on this occasion, as will be seen later. Our distance that day (December 4) was close upon twenty-five miles; height above the sea, 20,100 feet.

The weather did not continue fine for long. Next day (December 5) there was a gale from the north, and once more the whole plain was a mass of drifting snow. In addition to this there was thick falling snow, which blinded us and made things worse, but a feeling of security had come over us and helped us to advance rapidly and without hesitation, although we could see nothing. That day we encountered new surface conditions—big, hard snow waves (sastrugi). These were anything but pleasant to work among, especially when one could not see them. It was of no use for us "forerunners" to think of going in advance under these circumstances, as it was impossible to keep on one's feet. Three or four paces was often the most we managed to do before falling down. The *sastrugi* were very high, and often abrupt; if one came on them unexpectedly, one required to be more than an acrobat to keep on one's feet. The plan we found to work best in these conditions was to let Hanssen's dogs go first; this was an unpleasant job for Hanssen, and for his dogs too, but it succeeded, and succeeded well. An upset here and there was, of course, unavoidable, but with a little patience the sledge was always righted again. The drivers had as much as they could do to support their sledges among the *sastrugi*, but while supporting the sledges, they had at the same time a support for themselves. It was worse for us who had no sledges, but by keeping in the wake of them we could see where the irregularities lay, and thus get over them. Hanssen deserves a special word of praise for his driving on this surface in such weather. It is a difficult matter to drive Eskimo dogs forward when they cannot see; but Hanssen managed it well, both getting the dogs on and steering his course by compass. One would not think it possible to keep an approximately right course when the uneven ground gives such violent shocks that the needle flies several times round the compass, and is no sooner still again than it recommences the same dance; but when at last we got an observation, it turned out that Hanssen had steered to a hair, for the observations and dead reckoning agreed to a mile. In spite of all hindrances, and of being able to see nothing, the sledge meters showed nearly twenty-five miles. The hypsometer showed 11,070 feet above the sea; we had therefore reached a greater altitude than the Butcher's.

December 6 brought the same weather: thick snow, sky and plain all one, nothing to be seen. Nevertheless we made splendid progress. The *sastrugi* gradually became leveled out, until the surface was perfectly smooth; it was a relief to have even ground to go upon once more. These irregularities that one was constantly falling over were a nuisance; if we had met with them in our usual surroundings it would not have mattered so much; but up here on the high ground, where we had to stand and gasp for breath every time we rolled over, it was certainly not pleasant.

That day we passed 88° S., and camped in 88° 9′ S. A great surprise awaited us in the tent that evening. I expected to find, as on the previous evening, that the boiling point had fallen somewhat; in other words, that it would show a continued rise of the ground, but to our astonishment this was not so. The water boiled at exactly the same temperature as on the preceding day. I tried it several times, to convince myself that there was nothing wrong, each time with the same results. There was great rejoicing among us all when I was able to announce that we had arrived on the top of the plateau.

December 7 began like the 6th, with absolutely thick weather, but, as they say, you never know what the day is like before sunset. Possibly I might have chosen a better expression than this last—one more in agreement with the natural conditions—but I will let it stand. Though for several weeks now the sun had not set, my readers will not be so critical as to reproach me with inaccuracy. With a light wind from the northeast, we now went southward at a good speed over the perfectly level plain, with excellent going. The uphill work had taken it out of our dogs, though not to any serious extent. They had turned greedy—there is no denying that—and the half kilo of pemmican they got each day was not enough to fill their stomachs. Early and late they were looking for something—no matter what—to devour. To begin with they contented themselves with such loose objects as ski bindings, whips, boots, and the like; but as we came to know their proclivities, we took such care of everything that they found no extra meals lying about. But that was not the end of the matter. They then went for the fixed lashings of the sledges, and—if we had allowed it—would very quickly have resolved the various sledges into their component parts. But we found a way of stopping that: every evening, on halting, the sledges were buried in the snow, so as to hide all the lashings. That was successful; curiously enough, they never tried to force the "snow rampart."

I may mention as a curious thing that these ravenous animals, that devoured everything they came across, even to the ebonite points of our ski sticks, never made any attempt to break into the provision cases. They lay there and went about among the sledges with their noses just on a level with the split cases, seeing and scenting the pemmican, without once making a sign of taking any. But if one raised a lid, they were not long in showing themselves. Then they all came in a great hurry and flocked about the sledges in the hope of getting a little extra bit. I am at a loss to explain this behavior; that bashfulness was not at the root of it, I am tolerably certain.

During the forenoon the thick, gray curtain of cloud began to grow thinner on the horizon, and for the first time for three days we could see a few miles about us. The feeling was something like that one has on waking from a good nap, rubbing one's eyes and looking around. We had become so accustomed to the gray twilight that this positively dazzled us. Meanwhile, the upper layer of air seemed obstinately to remain the same and to be doing its best to prevent the sun from showing itself. We badly wanted to get a meridian altitude, so that we could determine our latitude. Since 86° 47′ S. we had had no observation, and it was not easy to say when we should get one. Hitherto, the weather conditions on the high ground had not been particularly favorable. Although the prospects were not very promising, we halted at 11 A.M. and made ready to catch the sun if it should be kind enough to look out. Hassel and Wisting used one sextant and artificial horizon, Hanssen and I the other set.

I don't know that I have ever stood and absolutely pulled at the sun to get it out as I did that time. If we got an observation here which agreed with our reckoning, then it would be possible, if the worst came to the worst, to go to the Pole on dead reckoning; but if we got none now, it was a question whether our claim to the Pole would be admitted on the dead reckoning we should be able to produce. Whether my pulling helped or not, it is certain that the sun appeared. It was not very brilliant to begin with, but, practiced as we now were in availing ourselves of even the poorest chances, it was good enough. Down it came, was checked by all, and the altitude written down. The curtain of cloud was rent more and more, and before we had finished our work—that is to say, caught the sun at its highest, and convinced ourselves that it was descending again—it was shining in all its glory. We had put away our instruments and were sitting on the sledges, engaged in the calculations. I can safely say that we were excited. What would the result be, after marching blindly for so long and over such impossible ground, as we had been doing? We added and subtracted, and at last there was the result. We looked at each other in sheer incredulity: the result was as astonishing as the most consummate conjuring trick—88° 16′ S., precisely to a minute the same as our reckoning, 88° 16′ S. If we were forced to go to the Pole on dead reckoning, then surely the most exacting would admit our right to do so. We put away our observation books, ate one or two biscuits, and went at it again.

We had a great piece of work before us that day: nothing less than carrying our flag farther south than the foot of man had trod. We had our silk flag ready; it was made fast to two ski sticks and laid on Hanssen's sledge. I had given him orders that as soon as we had covered the distance to 88° 23′ S., which was Shackleton's farthest south, the flag was to be hoisted on his sledge. It was my turn as forerunner, and I pushed on. There was no longer any difficulty in holding one's course; I had the grandest cloud formations to steer by, and everything now went like a machine. First came the forerunner for the time being, then Hanssen, then Wisting, and finally Bjaaland. The forerunner who was not on duty went where he liked; as a rule he accompanied one or other of the sledges. I had long ago fallen into a reverie—far removed from the scene in which I was moving; what I thought about I do not remember now, but I was so preoccupied that I had entirely forgotten my surroundings. Then suddenly I was roused from my dreaming by a jubilant shout, followed by ringing cheers. I turned round quickly to discover the reason of this unwonted occurrence, and stood speechless and overcome.

I find it impossible to express the feelings that possessed me at this moment. All the sledges had stopped, and from the foremost of them the Norwegian flag was flying. It shook itself out, waved and flapped so that the silk rustled; it looked wonderfully well in the pure, clear air and the shining white surroundings. 88° 23′ was past; we were farther south than any human being had been. No other moment of the whole trip affected me like this. The tears forced their way to my eyes; by no effort of will could I keep them back. It was the flag yonder that conquered me and my will. Luckily I was some way in advance of the others, so that I had time to pull myself together and master my feelings before reaching my comrades. . . .

After much consideration and discussion we had come to the conclusion that we ought to lay down a depot—the last one—at this spot. The advantages of lightening our sledges were so great that we should have to risk it. Nor would there be any great risk attached to it, after all, since we should adopt a system of marks that would lead even a blind man back to the place. We had determined to mark it not only at right angles to our course—that is, from east to west—but by snow beacons at every two geographical miles to the south.

We stayed here on the following day to arrange this depot.

Hanssen's dogs were real marvels, all of them; nothing seemed to have any effect on them. They had grown rather thinner, of course, but they were still as strong as ever. It was therefore decided not to lighten Hanssen's sledge, but only the two others; both Wisting's and Bjaaland's teams had suffered, especially the latter's. The reduction in weight that was effected was considerable—nearly 110 pounds on each of the two sledges; there was thus about 220 pounds in the depot. The snow here was ill-adapted for building, but we put up quite a respectable monument all the same. It was dogs' pemmican and biscuits that were left behind; we carried with us on the sledges provisions for about a month. If, therefore, contrary to expectation, we should be so unlucky as to miss this depot, we should nevertheless be fairly sure of reaching our depot in 86° 21′ before supplies ran short. The cross-marking of the depot was done with sixty splinters of black packing case on each side, with 100 paces between each. Every other one had a shred of black cloth on the top. The splinters on the east side were all marked, so that on seeing them we should know instantly that we were to the east of the depot. Those on the west had no marks.

The warmth of the past few days seemed to have matured our frost sores, and we presented an awful appearance. It was Wisting, Hanssen, and I who had suffered the worst damage in the last southeast blizzard; the left side of our faces was one mass of sore, bathed in matter and serum. We looked like the worst type of tramps and ruffians, and would probably not have been recognized by our nearest relations. These sores were a great trouble to us during the latter part of the journey. The slightest gust of wind produced a sensation as if one's face were being cut backward and forward with a blunt knife. They lasted a long time, too; I can remember Hanssen removing the last scab when we were coming into Hobart—three months later. We were very lucky in the weather during this depot work; the sun came out all at once, and we had an excellent opportunity of taking some good azimuth observations, the last of any use that we got on the journey.

December 9 arrived with the same fine weather and sunshine. True, we felt our frost sores rather sharply that day, with —18.4° F. and a little breeze dead against us, but that could not be helped. We at once began to put up beacons—a work which was continued with great regularity right up to the Pole.

These beacons were not so big as those we had built down on the Barrier; we could see that they would be quite large enough with a height of about 3 feet, as it was very easy to see the slightest irregularity on this perfectly flat surface. While thus engaged we had an opportunity of becoming thoroughly acquainted with the nature of the snow. Often—very often indeed—on this part of the plateau, to the south of 88° 25′, we had difficulty in getting snow good enough—that is, solid enough for cutting blocks. The snow up here seemed to have fallen very quietly, in light breezes or calms. We could thrust the tent pole, which was 6 feet long, right down without meeting resistance, which showed that there was no hard layer of snow. The surface was also perfectly level; there was not a sign of *sastrugi* in any direction.

Every step we now took in advance brought us rapidly nearer the goal; we could feel fairly certain of reaching it on the afternoon of the 14th. It was very natural that our conversation should be chiefly concerned with the time of arrival. None of us would admit that he was nervous, but I am inclined to think that we all had a little touch of that malady. What should we see when we got there? A vast, endless plain, that no eye had yet seen and no foot yet trodden; or—No, it was an impossibility; with the speed at which we had traveled, we must reach the goal first, there could be no doubt about that. And yet—and yet—Wherever there is the smallest loophole, doubt creeps in and gnaws and gnaws and never leaves a poor wretch in peace. "What on earth is Uroa scenting? It was Bjaaland who made this remark, on one of these last days, when I was going by the side of his sledge and talking to him. "And the strange thing is that he's scenting to the south. It can never be—" Myliuns, Ring, and Suggen showed the same interest in the southerly direction; it was quite extraordinary to see how they raised their heads, with every sign of curiosity, put their noses in the air, and sniffed due south. One would really have thought there was something remarkable to be found there.

From 88° 25′ S. the barometer and hypsometer indicated slowly but surely that the plateau was beginning to descend toward the other side.

This was a pleasant surprise to us; we had thus not only found the very summit of the plateau, but also the slope down on the far side. This would have a very important bearing for obtaining an idea of the construction of the whole plateau. On December 9 observations and dead reckoning agreed within a mile. The same result again on the 10th: observation 2 kilometers behind reckoning. The weather and going remained about the same as on the preceding days: light southeasterly breeze, temperature —18.4° F. The snow surface was loose, but ski and sledges glided over it well. On the 11th, the same weather conditions. Temperature —13° F. Observation and reckoning again agreed exactly. Our latitude was 89° 15′ S. On the 12th we reached 89° 30′, reckoning 1 kilometer behind observation. Going and surface as good as ever. Weather splendid—calm with sunshine. The noon observation on the 13th gave 89° 37′ S. Reckoning 89° 38.5′ S. We halted in the afternoon, after going eight geographical miles, and camped in 89° 45′, according to reckoning.

The weather during the forenoon had been just as fine as before; in the afternoon we had some snow showers from the southeast. It was like the eve of some great festival that night in the tent. One could feel that a great event was at hand. Our flag was taken out again and lashed to the same two ski sticks as before. Then it was rolled up and laid aside, to be ready when the time came. I was awake several times during the night, and had the same feeling that I can remember as a little boy on the night before Christmas Eve—an intense expectation of what was going to happen. Otherwise I think we slept just as well that night as any other.

On the morning of December 14 the weather was of the finest, just as if it had been made for arriving at the Pole. I am not quite sure, but I believe we dispatched our breakfast rather more quickly than usual and were out of the tent sooner, though I must admit that we always accomplished this with all reasonable haste. We went in the usual order—the forerunner, Hanssen, Wisting, Bjaaland, and the reserve forerunner. By noon we had reached 89° 53′ by dead reckoning, and made ready to take the rest in one stage. At 10 A.M. a light breeze had sprung up from the southeast, and it had clouded over, so that we got no noon altitude; but the clouds were not thick, and from time to time we had a glimpse of the sun through them. The going on that day was rather different from what it had been; sometimes the ski went over it well, but at others it was pretty bad. We advanced that day in the same mechanical way as before; not much was said, but eyes were used all the more. Hanssen's neck grew twice as long as before in his endeavor to see a few inches farther. I had asked him before we started to spy out ahead for all he was worth, and he did so with a vengeance. But, however keenly he stared, he could not descry anything but the endless flat plain ahead of us. The dogs had dropped their scenting, and appeared to have lost their interest in the regions about the earth's axis.

At three in the afternoon a simultaneous "Halt" rang out from the drivers. They had carefully examined their sledge meters, and they all showed the full distance—our Pole by reckoning. The goal was reached, the journey ended. I cannot say—though I know it would sound much more effective—that the object of my life was attained. That would be romancing rather too barefacedly. I had better be honest and admit straight out that I have never known any man to be placed in such a diametrically opposite position to the goal of his desires as I was at that moment. The regions around the North Pole—well, yes, the North Pole itself—had attracted me from childhood, and here I was at the South Pole. Can anything more topsy-turvy be imagined?

We reckoned now that we were at the Pole. Of course, every one of us knew that we were not standing on the absolute spot; it would be an impossibility with the time and the instruments at our disposal to ascertain that exact spot. But we were so near it that the few miles which possibly separated us from it could not be of the slightest importance. It was our intention to make a circle round this camp, with a radius of twelve and a half miles, and to be satisfied with that. After we had halted we collected and congratulated each other. We had good grounds for mutual respect in what had been achieved, and I think that was just the feeling that was expressed in the firm and powerful grasps of the fist that were exchanged. After this we proceeded to the greatest and most solemn act of the whole journey—the planting of our flag. Pride and affection shone in the five pairs of eyes that gazed upon the flag, as it unfurled itself with a sharp crack, and waved over the Pole. I had determined that the act of planting it—the historic event—should be equally divided among us all. It was not for one man to do this; it was for *all* who had staked their lives in the struggle, and held together through thick and thin. This was the only way in which I could show my gratitude to my comrades in this desolate spot. I could see that they understood and accepted it in the spirit in which it was offered. Five weatherbeaten, frostbitten fists they were that grasped the pole, raised the waving flag in the air, and planted it as the first at the geographical South Pole. "Thus we plant thee, beloved flag, at the South Pole, and give to the plain on which it lies the name of King Haakon VII's Plateau." That moment will certainly be remembered by all of us who stood there.

One gets out of the way of protracted ceremonies in those regions—the shorter they are the better. Everday life began again at once.

TWO in the GREAT NORTH WOODS

BETH DAY

Jim and Laurette Stanton, bored by life in Seattle, where Jim ran a garage business, decided to explore the wilderness together. They sold the business, pocketed the money, and headed for the north woods. In Vancouver they bought a boat and supplies and embarked on a long fishing trip from which they never returned. Although life in the wild was hard—trapping, fishing, logging, and contending with grizzly bears, they never regretted the experience of being latter-day pioneers.

Here is how they started out, as told by Beth Day in her book, Grizzlies in Their Back Yard, *New York: Julian Messner, 1956.*

One warm, windy day in late June, 1919, a small double-ended rowboat, powered by a 2½-horsepower kicker engine, threaded its way among the maze of channels and islands in Queen Charlotte Strait, which separates Vancouver Island from the mountainous western coast of British Columbia. At the tiller was Jim Stanton, a short, wiry, auburn-haired young man with a tip-tilted Scotch nose and observant blue eyes, etched by squint-lines.

Beside him sat his boyishly slender wife, Laurette, brown hair pushed under an old fishing cap, widely spaced brown eyes fixed eagerly on the rolling emerald water which parted before their boat.

Along with complete fishing equipment for casting and trolling, they carried a balloon-silk tent so that they could camp ashore. Jim had his 30-30 rifle and plenty of ammunition. Their staple foods were packed in watertight tins; they had canned heat, and a lazy board to lean against so they could eat their meals aboard while anchored in a sheltered cove.

Suddenly two channels appeared before them; Jim let go of the rudder, leaving the boat to choose its own course. Putting an arm around her, he pulled Laurette down with him behind the spray hood which was battened over the fore two-thirds of their boat.

The small craft hesitated momentarily where the two channels met, shuddered in the cross currents, and then, leaving Seymour Narrows, the main steam channel to Alaska, it swerved right and plunged toward the high blue mountains ahead.

"That's wild country up there," Jim said, pointing. "Are you game?"

The water had quieted and Laurette stood up, flinging out her arms. "It's glorious!"

"Grizzly country, maybe."

"You and your grizzlies! But Jim," she said thoughtfully, "I have a feeling that we'll find what we're looking for here."

"There'll be hardship, too," he reminded her. "We haven't much money, you know."

"If we'd waited until we did, we'd still be back in Seattle. We took a chance, and I'm glad!"

"A mighty big chance, dear." Jim laid a hand on the rudder again, steadying it. "I've got to find some way to make a living; and we need a roof and a fire before winter sets in."

"Meanwhile," Laurette said contentedly, "we can fish and dream."

A week later they stopped at one of the fish cannery stores, which are found along the British Columbia coast line, for the rare luxury of a real meal. . . . The cannery man told them that the best place for trout was Lake Atluck, so, following his directions, they pushed up the Nimpkish River, a trip that took three days. On the way they went through thirty-six rapids in six miles; Laurette lined the boat from the bank, and Jim, waist-deep in the white, boiling water, guided it clear of the rocks.

At last they were able to make camp and rest on the shore of the wild, lovely little lake. The first morning they awoke to discover that they had had a visitor during the night. Fresh cougar tracks circled their silk tent. Every morning for two weeks they saw new tracks, but not once did they meet the curious cautious cat.

There were no other camps on the lake, but Jim had the distinct feeling that they and the cougar were not its only inhabitants.

"Someone's in here," he told Laurette, "and they don't want to meet us."

Laurette scoffed at the notion, but Jim's ears had not deceived him. Late one night he shook Laurette awake.

"Listen!" he whispered. "Oarlocks. Someone is out on the lake right now."

The next morning Jim found a splash of blood on a log. "I think it's trappers," he said. "I wonder why they're hiding from us?"

That afternoon he made a complete circuit of the lake, gliding swiftly yet soundlessly through the woods, the way he had been taught years before. "You learn to walk in the woods," Jim explained to Laurette, "as you learn to dance. You look ten feet ahead of you and then advance. Your mind records every obstruction before you, and you automatically step over them without making any noise."

Jim found the trappers in their camp hidden deep in the woods—two giant, black-bearded brothers who dwarfed Jim's scant five feet six inches. When they saw that Jim was friendly, they told him their story.

They were Alaskan sourdoughs, nicknamed Baldy and Bones. They had, they said, trapped in Alaska for two years until they had accumulated a big pile of furs. Their gear was packed and they were ready to go when they spotted a grizzly. Getting their guns, they headed after him.

They got their bear, but when they returned to camp they found that it had burned to the ground. A spark from the breakfast fire had evidently blown on their gear. For their two years of hard work they now had nothing but the clothes on their backs and their guns. They had then left Alaska and wandered down into British Columbia. When they found Lake Atluck without a soul on it, they settled down to trap for a season. (There were no registered trap lines then; a man was free to trap anywhere he took a notion to.) When the Stantons appeared on the lake, the sourdoughs naturally assumed that they were trappers who had come to horn in on them.

Jim assured them that he and Laurette weren't trapping, and took the two bearded giants back to his camp to meet Laurette.

"A woman!" they exclaimed in unison.

They had spied on the newcomers; the sourdoughs admitted what Jim already knew. But in her fishing pants and shirt, with a cap pulled down over her hair, they had figured that Laurette was a boy.

They had seen so few women in recent years that they were clumsily unsure of how to act. But when Laurette offered them fresh home made bread, with butter and jam, and hot tea, they relaxed, and swapped information with Jim.

"We went up into Knight Inlet," Bones told them. "Heard that's the wildest spot in British Columbia. But it was too wild for us. Too many grizzlies up there."

"Grizzlies!" Jim felt a familiar prickle of hair on the back of his neck.

"Grizzlies!" Laurette echoed. "Knight Inlet, you say? Well, that's where we're going. Right, Jim?"

"Don't know as it's any place for a woman," Baldy said. "Nobody lives on the Inlet regular. A few Indians come up in spring for the oolachan run; some in the fall to trap. But nobody lives there permanent—'cept for the watchman they leave at the cannery at Glendale."

"We don't mind being alone," Laurette said.

They headed down the Nimpkish River for Knight Inlet. Though it had taken them three days to make the run upriver, they whipped down in only two hours. At Johnstone Strait, they confidently headed toward the mouth of the Inlet. Halfway, they hit a cross sea and their heavily laden boat suddenly began to fill.

They finally reached the lee of one of the many islands which clog the strait, and were able to rest for a few minutes. Then they went out again into the wild water and fought their way toward the mouth of the Inlet, where Baldy and Bones had told them they could get fresh supplies.

Minstrel Island, however, was deserted, and the frame hotel building they had seen from the water proved to be empty.

There was nothing, the sourdoughs had informed them, from Minstrel Island to Glendale Cove, a third of the way up the Inlet; then nothing from Glendale to the Head, where there was an Indian camp. Finally, they reached Glendale, where a fish cannery was open and a store which supplied the itinerant fishermen, hand loggers, and Indians who came into the Inlet during the warm months of the year.

By this time it was dusk, so after hastily loading in meat and groceries, they went upstream looking for a place to camp.

The next morning they awoke to a veritable paradise. From their secluded bay they looked out at a magnificent, untouched world. Before them, deep glacial water wound between pine-covered shores for miles. Snow-covered peaks rose twelve thousand feet and more. Natural waterfalls striped the dark forest with silver ribbons. The Inlet water itself was a mysterious opaque green, colored by the flow from the great ice fields above.

They cruised slowly up Knight Inlet toward its head. Virgin timber and unclimbed mountains stretched before them endlessly. Giant pillars of trees rose hundreds of feet into the air. There was a strangely silent, primeval quality to the forest and shores.

Jim pointed across to the western shore, at a point about six miles from Glendale.

"Look over there, dear. Looks like an abandoned cabin. Bet it's a trapper's or logger's place. Probably nobody's lived there for years."

And when they pulled in to the beach, they found that Jim had been right; it was deserted. A solidly built, one-room logger's cabin, it was made of cedar shakes, and the roof was still sound. The interior was a tangled mass of leaves interlaced with mouse trails.

"Well, it's not exactly a palace," Laurette said, "but it would be better than a silk tent in the winter."

"Looks solid enough," Jim said. "And I could fix it up a little —that is, if you want to stay."

It was as simple as that.

PART IV

Stalkers and Fugitives of the Wilds

ARCTIC RENDEZVOUS

RACHEL CARSON

—a selection from Rachel Carson's Under the Sea-Wind, *New York: Oxford University Press, Inc., 1941.*

The late Rachel Carson became widely known for her book, Silent Spring, *which warned of the terrible devastation possible as a result of the uncurbed use of insecticides by man. In her earlier work,* Under the Sea-Wind, *she depicted the migration of a flock of sanderlings. Her description of birds in the Arctic shows that nature herself is terrible, with one species of animal preying on another, and hunger a most frightening aspect of the wild in winter. In the excerpt presented here, recounting the relentless pursuit of ptarmigan by a snowy owl, the elements are sublimely impartial, camouflaging bird of prey and victim alike with a background of snow.*

The sanderlings faced into the blizzard, as shore birds everywhere face into the wind. They huddled close together, wing to wing, and the warmth of their bodies kept the tender feet from freezing as they crouched on them.

If the snow had not drifted so, that night and all the next day, the loss of life would have been less. But the stream valleys filled up, inch by inch, throughout the night, and against the ridges the white softness piled deeper. Little by little, from the ice-strewn sea edge across miles of tundra, even far south to the fringe of the forests, the undulating hills and the ice-scoured valleys were flattening out, and a strange world, terrifying in its level whiteness, was building up. In the purple twilight of the second day the fall slackened, and the night was loud with the crying of the wind, but with no other voice, for no wild thing dared show itself.

The snow death had taken many lives. It had visited the nest of two snowy owls in a ravine that cut a deep scar in the hillside, near the willow copse that sheltered the sanderlings. The hen had been brooding the six eggs for more than a week. During the first night of wild storm the snow had drifted deep about her, leaving a round depression like a stream-bed pothole in which she sat. All through the night the owl remained on the nest, warming the eggs with her great body that was almost furry in its plumage. By morning the snow was filling in around the feather-shod talons and creeping up around her sides. The cold was numbing, even through the feathers. At noon, with flakes like cotton shreds still flying in the sky, only the owl's head and shoulders were free of the snow. Several times that day a great form, white and silent as the snowflakes, had drifted over the ridge and hovered above the place where the nest was. Now Ookpik, the cock owl, called to his mate with low, throaty cries. Numb and heavy-winged with cold, the hen roused and shook herself. It took many minutes to free herself from the snow and to climb, half fluttering, half stumbling, out of the nest, deep-walled with white. Ookpik clucked to her and made the sounds of a cock owl bringing a lemming or a baby ptarmigan to the nest, but neither owl had had food since the blizzard began. The hen tried to fly but her heavy body flopped awkwardly in the snow for stiffness. When at last the slow circulation had crept back into her muscles, she rose into the air and the two owls floated over the place where the sanderlings crouched and out across the tundra.

As the snow fell on the still-warm eggs and the hard, bitter cold of the night gripped them, the life fires of the tiny embryos burned low. The crimson streams ran slower in the vessels that carried the racing blood from the food yolks to the embryos. After a time there slackened and finally ceased the furious activity of cells that grew and divided, grew again and divided to make owl bone and muscle and sinew. The pulsating red sacs under the great oversized heads hesitated, beat spasmodically, and were stilled. The six little owls-to-be were dead in the snow, and by their death, perhaps, hundreds of unborn lemmings and ptarmigans and Arctic hares had the greater chance of escaping death from the feathered ones that strike from the sky.

Farther up the ravine, several willow ptarmigans had been buried in a drift, where they had bedded for the night. The ptarmigans had flown over the ridge on the evening of the storm, dropping into the soft drifts so that never a print of their feet—

clad in feathered snowshoes—was left to guide the foxes to their resting place. This was a rule of the game of life and death which the weak play with the strong. But tonight there was no need to observe the rules, for the snow would have obliterated all footprints and would have outwitted the keenest enemy—even as it drifted, by slow degrees, so deeply over the sleeping ptarmigans that they could not dig themselves out.

Five of the sanderling flock had died of the cold, and snow buntings by the score were stumbling and fluttering over the snow crust, too weak to stand when they tried to alight.

Now, with the passing of the storm, hunger was abroad on the great barrens. Most of the willows, food of the ptarmigans, were buried under snow. The dried heads of last year's weeds, which released their seeds to the snow buntings and the longspurs, wore glittering sheaths of ice. The lemmings, food of the foxes and the owls, were safe in their runways, and nowhere in this silent world was there food for shore birds that live on the shellfish and insects and other creatures of the water's edge. Now many hunters, both furred and feathered, were abroad during the night, the short, gray night of the Arctic spring. And when night wore into day the hunters still padded over the snow or beat on strong wings across the tundra, for the night's kill had not satisfied their hunger.

Among the hunters was Ookpik, the snowy owl. The coldest months of every winter, the icebound months, Ookpik spent hundreds of miles south of the barren grounds, where it was easier to find the little gray lemming mice that were his favorite food. During the storm nothing living had showed itself to Ookpik as he sailed over the plains and along the ridges that overlooked the sea, but today many small creatures moved over the tundra.

Along the east bank of the stream a flock of ptarmigans had found a few twigs of willow showing above the snow, part of a shrubby growth that had been as high as the antlers of a barren-grounds caribou until the snow had covered it. Now the ptarmigans could easily reach the topmost branches, and they nipped off the twigs in their bills, content with this food until the tender new buds of spring should be put forth. The flock still wore the white plumage of winter except for one or two of the cocks whose few brown feathers told of approaching summer and the mating season. When a ptarmigan in winter dress feeds on the snow fields, all of color about him is the black of bill and roving eye, and of the under tail feathers when he flies. Even his ancient enemies, the foxes and the owls, are deceived from a distance; but they, too, wear the Arctic's protective colorings.

Now Ookpik, as he came up the stream valley, saw among the willows the moving balls of shining black that were the ptarmigans' eyes. The white foe moved nearer, blending into the pale sky; the white prey moved, unfrightened, over the snow. There was a soft *whoosh* of wings—a scattering of feathers—and on the snow a red stain spread, red as a new-laid ptarmigan egg before the shell pigments have dried. Ookpik bore the ptarmigan in his talons over the ridge to the higher ground that was his lookout, where his mate awaited him. The two owls tore apart the warm flesh with their beaks, swallowing also the bones and feathers as was their custom, to cast them up later in neat pellets.

THE BUFFALO CHASE

FRANCIS PARKMAN

—a selection from The Oregon Trail *(1849), by Francis Parkman.*

Francis Parkman was a frail Bostonian who traveled from St. Louis to Fort Laramie, Wyoming, and lived for several weeks with the Sioux Indians. His book, The Oregon Trail, *became a classic of American frontier life when the United States was still a wilderness, overrun with wild animals. The episode presented here is an exciting account of hunting the American bison in the days when they were plentiful enough to blacken the plains as far as the eye could see.*

The next day was one of activity and excitement, for about ten o'clock the man in advance shouted the gladdening cry of "Buffalo! Buffalo!" and in the hollow of the prairie just below us a band of bulls were grazing. The temptation was irresistible and Shaw and I rode down upon them. We were badly mounted on our traveling horses, but by hard lashing we overtook them, and Shaw, running alongside a bull, shot into him both balls of his double-barreled gun. Looking round as I galloped by, I saw the bull in his mortal fury rushing again and again upon his antagonist, whose horse constantly leaped aside and avoided the onset. My chase was more protracted, but at length I ran close to the bull and killed him with my pistols. Cutting off the tails of our victims by way of trophy, we rejoined the party in about a quarter of an hour after we had left it. Again and again that morning rang out the same welcome cry of "Buffalo! Buffalo!" Every few moments, in the broad meadows along the river, we saw bands of bulls, who, raising their shaggy heads, would gaze in stupid amazement at the approaching horsemen, and then, breaking into a clumsy gallop, file off in a long line across the trail in front, toward the rising prairie on the left. At noon the plain before us was alive with thousands of buffalo, bulls, cows, and calves, all moving rapidly as we drew near; and far off beyond the river the swelling prairie was darkened with them to the very horizon. The party was in gayer spirits than ever. We stopped for a nooning near a grove of trees by the river.

"Tongues and hump ribs tomorrow," said Shaw, looking with contempt at the venison steaks which Deslauriers placed before us. Our meal finished, we lay down to sleep. A shout from Henry Chatillon aroused us, and we saw him standing on the cart wheel, stretching his tall figure to its full height while he looked toward the prairie beyond the river. Following the direction of his eyes, we could clearly distinguish a large dark object, like the black shadow of a cloud, passing rapidly over swell after swell of the distant plain; behind it followed another of similar appearance though smaller, moving more rapidly, and drawing closer and closer to the first. It was the hunters of the Arapahoe camp chasing a band of buffalo. Shaw and I caught and saddled our best horses and went plunging through sand and water to the farther bank. We were too late. The hunters had already mingled with the herd, and the work of slaughter was nearly over. When we reached the ground we found it strewn far and near with numberless carcasses, while the remnants of the herd, scattered in all directions, were flying away in terror, and the Indians still rushing in pursuit. Many of the hunters, however, remained upon the spot, and among the rest was our yesterday's acquaintance, the chief of the village. He had alighted by the side of a cow, into which he had shot five or six arrows, and his squaw, who had followed him on horseback to the hunt, was giving him a draught of water from a canteen purchased or plundered from some volunteer soldier. Recrossing the river, we overtook the party, who were already on their way.

We had gone scarcely a mile when we saw an imposing spectacle. From the river bank on the right, away over the swelling prairie on the left, and in front as far as the eye could reach, was one vast host of buffalo. The outskirts of the herd were within a quarter of a mile. In many parts they were crowded so densely together that in the distance their rounded backs presented a surface of uniform blackness; but elsewhere they were more scattered, and from amid the multitude rose little columns of dust where some of them were rolling on the ground. Here and there a battle was going forward among the bulls. We could distinctly see them rushing against each other, and hear the clattering of their horns and their hoarse bellowing. Shaw was riding at some distance in advance, with Henry Chatillon; I saw him stop and draw the leather covering from his gun. With such a sight before us, but one thing could be thought of. That morning I had used pistols in the chase. I had now a mind to try the virtue of a gun. Deslauriers had one, and I rode up to the side of the cart; there he sat under the white covering, biting his pipe between his teeth and grinning with excitement.

"Lend me your gun, Deslauriers."

"Oui, Monsieur, oui," said Deslauriers, tugging with might and main to stop the mule, which seemed obstinately bent on going forward. Then everything but his moccasins disappeared as he crawled into the cart and pulled at the gun to extricate it.

"Is it loaded?" I asked.

"Oui, bien chargé; you'll kill, mon bourgeois; yes, you'll kill—c'est un bon fusil."

I handed him my rifle and rode forward to Shaw.

"Are you ready?" he asked.

"Come on," said I.

"Keep down that hollow," said Henry, "and then they won't see you till you get close to them."

The hollow was a kind of wide ravine; it ran obliquely toward the buffalo, and we rode at a canter along the bottom until it became too shallow; then we bent close to our horses' necks, and, at last, finding that it could no longer conceal us, came out of it and rode directly toward the herd. It was within gunshot; before its outskirts numerous grizzly old bulls were scattered, holding guard over their females. They glared at us in anger and astonishment, walked toward us a few yards, and then, turning slowly round, retreated at a trot which afterward broke into a clumsy gallop. In an instant the main body caught the alarm. The buffalo began to crowd away from the point toward which we were approaching, and a gap was opened in the side of the herd. We entered it, still restraining our excited horses. Every instant the tumult was thickening. The buffalo, pressing together in large bodies, crowded away from us on every hand. In front and on either side we could see dark columns and masses, half hidden by clouds of dust, rushing along in terror and confusion, and hear the tramp and clattering of ten thousand hoofs. That countless multitude of powerful brutes, ignorant of their own strength, were flying in a panic from the approach of two feeble horsemen. To remain quiet longer was impossible.

"Take that band on the left," said Shaw. "I'll take these in front."

He sprang off and I saw no more of him. A heavy Indian whip, or "quirt," was fastened by a band to my wrist; I swung it into the air and lashed my horse's flank with all the strength of my arm. Away she darted, stretching close to the ground. I could see nothing but a cloud of dust before me but I knew that it concealed a band of many hundreds of buffalo. In a moment I was in the midst of the cloud, half suffocated by the dust and stunned by the trampling of the flying herd; but I was drunk with the chase and cared for nothing but the buffalo. Very soon a long dark mass became visible, looming through the dust; then I could distinguish each bulky carcass, the hoofs flying out beneath, the short tails held rigidly erect. In a moment I was so close that I could have touched them with my gun.

Suddenly, to my amazement, the hoofs were jerked upward, the tails flourished in the air, and amid a cloud of dust the buffalo seemed to sink into the earth before me. One vivid impression of that instant remains upon my mind. I remember looking down upon the backs of several buffalo dimly visible through the dust. We had run unawares upon a ravine. At that moment I was not the most accurate judge of depth and width, but when I passed it on my return, I found it about twelve feet deep and not quite twice as wide at the bottom. It was impossible to stop; I would have done so gladly if I could; so, half sliding, half plunging, down went the little mare. She came down on her knees in the loose sand at the bottom; I was pitched forward against her neck and nearly thrown over her head among the buffalo, who amid dust and confusion came tumbling in all around. The mare was on her feet in an instant and scrambling like a cat up the opposite side. I thought for a moment that she would have fallen back and crushed me, but with a violent effort she clambered out and gained the hard prairie above.

Glancing back I saw the huge head of a bull clinging as it were by the forefeet at the edge of the dusty gulf. At length I was fairly among the buffalo. They were less densely crowded than before, and I could see nothing but bulls, who always run at the rear of herd to protect their females. As I passed among them they would lower their heads, and turning as they ran, try to gore my horse; but as they were already at full speed there was no force in their onset, and as Pauline ran faster than they, they were always thrown behind her in the effort.

I soon began to distinguish cows amid the throng. One just in front of me seemed to my liking, and I pushed close to her side. Dropping the reins I fired, holding the muzzle of the gun within a foot of her shoulder. Quick as lightning she sprang at Pauline; the little mare dodged the attack, and I lost sight of the wounded animal amid the tumult. Immediately after, I selected another, and urging forward Pauline, shot into her both pistols in succession. For a while I kept her in view, but in attempting to load my gun lost sight of her also in the confusion. Believing her to be mortally wounded and unable to keep up with the herd, I checked my horse.

The crowd rushed onward. The dust and tumult passed away, and on the prairie, far behind the rest, I saw a solitary buffalo galloping heavily. In a moment I and my victim were running side by side. My firearms were all empty, and I had in my pouch nothing but rifle bullets, too large for the pistols and too small for the gun. I loaded the gun, however, but as often as I leveled it to fire, the bullets would roll out of the muzzle and the gun returned only a report like a squib as the powder harmlessly exploded. I rode in front of the buffalo and tried to turn her back; but her eyes glared, her mane bristled and, lowering her head, she rushed at me with utmost fierceness and activity. Again and again I rode before her and again and again she repeated her furious charge. But little Pauline was in her element. She dodged her enemy at every rush, until at length the buffalo stood still, exhausted with her own efforts, her tongue lolling from her jaws.

Riding to a little distance, I dismounted, thinking to gather a handful of dry grass to serve the purpose of wadding, and load the gun at my leisure. No sooner were my feet on the ground than the buffalo came bounding in such a rage toward me that I jumped back again into the saddle with all possible despatch. After waiting a few minutes more, I made an attempt to ride up and stab her with my knife; but Pauline was near being gored in the attempt. At length, bethinking me of the fringes at the seams of my buckskin trousers, I jerked off a few of them and, reloading the gun, forced them down the barrel to keep the bullet in its place; then approaching, I shot the wounded buffalo through the heart. Sinking to her knees, she rolled over lifeless on the prairie. To my astonishment, I found that, instead of a cow, I had been slaughtering a stout young bull. No longer wondering at his fierceness, I opened his throat and, cutting out his tongue, tied it at the back of my saddle. My mistake was one which a more experienced eye than mine might easily make in the dust and confusion of such a chase.

Then for the first time I had leisure to look at the scene around me. The prairie in front was darkened with the retreating multitude, and on either hand the buffalo came filing up in endless columns from the low plains upon the river. The Arkansas was three or four miles distant. I turned and moved slowly toward it. A long time passed before, far in the distance, I distinguished the white covering of the cart and the little black specks of horsemen before and behind it. Drawing near, I recognized Shaw's elegant tunic, the red flannel shirt, conspicuous far off. I overtook the party and asked him what success he had had. He had assailed a fat cow, shot her with two bullets, and mortally wounded her. But neither of us was prepared for the chase that afternoon, and Shaw, like myself, had no spare bullets in his pouch; so he abandoned the disabled animal to Henry Chatillon, who followed, dispatched her with his rifle, and loaded his horse with the meat.

We encamped close to the river. The night was dark, and as we lay down we could hear, mingled with the howlings of wolves, the hoarse bellowing of the buffalo, like the ocean beating upon a distant coast.

A RACOON HUNT in KENTUCKY

JOHN JAMES AUDUBON

The racoon (or raccoon) is a North American native who makes an amusing pet or a wily adversary. It is in the latter character that John James Audubon portrays him in this vignette of a Kentucky racoon hunt, which is taken from the Ornithological Biography *(5 volumes, Edinburgh, 1831-39), which he coauthored with William MacGillivray.*

The Racoon, which is a cunning and crafty animal, is found in all our woods, so that its name is familiar to every child in the Union. The propensity which it evinces to capture all kinds of birds accessible to it in its nightly prowlings, for the purpose of feasting on their flesh, induces me to endeavour to afford you some idea of the pleasure which our western hunters feel in procuring it. With your leave, then, Reader, I will take you to a "Coon Hunt."

A few hours ago the sun went down far beyond the "far west." The woodland choristers have disappeared, the matron has cradled her babe, and betaken herself to the spinning-wheel; the woodsman, his sons, and "the stranger" are chatting before a blazing fire, making wise reflections on past events, and anticipating those that are to come. Autumn, sallow and sad, prepares to bow her head to the keen blast of approaching winter; . . . and each new morn has effected a gradual change in the dews, which now crust the withered herbage with a coat of glittering white. The sky is still cloudless; a thousand twinkling stars reflect their light from the tranquil waters; all is silent and calm in the forest, save the nightly prowlers that roam in its recesses. In the cheerful cabin all is happiness; its inmates generously strive to contribute to the comfort of the stranger who has chanced to visit them; and, as racoons are abundant in the neighbourhood, they propose a hunt. The offer is gladly accepted. The industrious woman leaves her wheel, for she has listened to her husband's talk; now she approaches the fire, takes up the board shovel, stirs the embers, produces a basket filled with sweet potatoes, arranges its contents side by side in front of the hearth, and covers them with hot ashes and glowing coals. All this she does, because she "guesses" that hungry stomachs will be calling for food when the sport is over. Ah! Reader, what "homely joys" there are in such scenes, and how you would enjoy them! The rich may produce a better, or a more sumptuous meal; but his feelings can never be like those of the poor woodsman. Poor I ought not to call him, for nature and industry bountifully supply all his wants; the woods and rivers produce his chief dainties, and his toils are his pleasures.

Now mark him! the bold Kentuckian is on his feet; his sons and the stranger prepare for the march. Horns and rifles are in requisition. The good man opens the wooden-hinged door, and sends forth a blast loud enough to scare a wolf. The racoons scamper away from the cornfields, break through the fences, and hie to the woods. The hunter has taken an axe from the wood-pile, and returning, assures us that the night is clear, and that we shall have rare sport. He blows through his rifle, to ascertain that it is clear, examines his flint, and thrusts a feather into the touch-hole. To a leathern bag swung at his side is attached a powder-horn; his sheathed knife is there also; below hangs a narrow strip of home-spun linen. He takes from his bag a bullet, pulls with his teeth the wooden stopper from his powder-horn, lays the ball on one hand, and with the other pours the powder upon it until it is just overtopped. Raising the horn to his mouth, he again closes it with the stopper, and restores it to its place. He introduces the powder into the tube; springs the box of his gun, greases the "patch" over with some melted tallow, or damps it; then places it on the honeycombed muzzle of his piece. The bullet is placed on the patch over the bore, and pressed with the handle of the knife, which now trims the edges of the linen. The elastic hickory rod, held with both hands, smoothly pushes the ball to its bed: once, twice, thrice has it rebounded. The rifle leaps as it were into the hunter's arms, the feather is drawn from the touch-hole, the powder fills the pan, which is closed. "Now

I'm ready," cries the woodsman. His companions say the same. Hardly more than a minute has elapsed. I wish, Reader, you had seen this fine fellow—but hark! the dogs are barking.

All is now bustle within and without: a servant lights a torch, and off we march to the woods. "Don't mind the boys, my dear sir," says the woodsman, "follow me close, for the ground is covered with logs, and the grape vines hang everywhere across." "Toby, hold up the light, man, or we'll never see the gullies." "Trail your gun, sir, as General Clark used to say,—not so, but this way—that's it; now then, no danger you see; no fear of snakes, poor things! They are stiff enough, I'll be bound. The dogs have treed one. Toby, you old fool, why don't you turn to the right—not so much there—go ahead, and give us light—What's that?— Who's there?— Ah, you young rascals! You've played us a trick, have you. It's all well enough, but now, just keep behind, or I'll"——and in fact, the boys, with eyes good enough to see in the dark, although not quite so well as an Owl's, had cut directly across the dogs, which had surprised a racoon on the ground and bayed it, until the lads knocked it on the head. "Seek him, boys," cries the hunter. —The dogs, putting their noses to the ground, pushed off at a good rate. "Master, they're making for the creek," says old Toby. On towards it therefore we push. What woods, to be sure! No gentleman's park this, I assure you, Reader. We are now in a low flat; the soil thinly covers the hard clay; nothing but beech trees hereabouts, unless now and then a maple. Hang the limbs! say I—hang the supple-jacks too—here I am, fast by the neck—cut it with your knife. My knee has had a tremendous rub against a log—now, my foot is jammed between two roots—and here I stick. "Toby, come back—don't you know the stranger is not up to the woods? Halloo, Toby, Toby!" There I stood perfectly shackled, the hunter laughing heartily, and the lads glad of an opportunity of slipping off. Toby arrived, and held the torch near the ground, on which the hunter cutting one of the roots with his hatchet, set me free. "Are you hurt, Sir?"—no, not in the least. Off we start again. The boys had got up with the dogs, which were baying a Racoon in a small puddle. We soon joined them with the light. "Now, stranger! watch and see!" The Racoon was all but swimming, and yet had hold of the bottom of the pool with his feet. The glare of the lighted torch was doubtless distressing to him;

his coat was ruffled, and his rounded tail seemed thrice its ordinary size, his eyes shone like emeralds; with foaming jaws he watched the dogs, ready to seize each by the snout if it came within reach. They kept him busy for several minutes; the water became thick with mud; his coat now hung dripping, and his draggled tail lay floating on the surface. His guttural growlings, in place of intimidating his assailants, excited them the more; and they very unceremoniously closed upon him, curs as they were, and without the breeding of gentle dogs! One seized him by the rump and tugged, but was soon forced to let go; another stuck to his side, but soon taking a better directed bite of his muzzle than another dog had just done of his tail, coon made him yelp; and pitiful were the cries of luckless Tyke. The Racoon would not let go, but in the mean time the other dogs seized him fast, and worried him to death, yet to the last he held by his antagonist's snout. Knocked on the head by an axe, he lay gasping his last breath, and the heaving of his chest was painful to see. The hunters stood gazing at him in the pool, while all around was by the flare of the torch rendered trebly dark and dismal. It was a good scene for a skilful painter.

We had now two coons, whose furs were worth two quarters of a dollar, and whose bodies, which I must not forget, as Toby informed us, would produce two more. "What now?" I asked—"What now?" quoth the father, "why go after more to be sure." So we did, the dogs ahead, and I far behind. In a short time the curs treed another, and when we came up, we found them seated on their haunches, looking upwards, and barking. The hunters now employed their axes, and sent the chips about at such a rate that one of them coming in contact with my cheek marked it so, that a week after several of my friends asked me where, in the name of wonder, I had got that black eye. At length the tree began to crack, and slowly leaning to one side, the heavy mass swung rustling through the air, and fell to the earth with a crash. It was not one coon that was surprised here, but three—aye three of them, one of which, more crafty than the rest, leaped fairly from the main top while the tree was staggering. The other two stuck to the hollow of a branch, from which they were soon driven by one of the dogs. Tyke and Lion having nosed the cunning old one, scampered after him, not mouthing like the well-trained hounds of our southern fox hunters, but yelling like furies. The hunter's sons attacked those on the tree, while the woodsman and I, preceeded by Toby, made after the other; and busy enough we all were. Our animal was of extraordinary size, and after some parley, a rifle ball was sent through his brain. He reeled once only,—next moment he lay dead. The rest were dispatched by the axe and the club, for a shot in those days was too valuable to be spent when it could be saved. It could procure a deer, and therefore was worth more than a coon's skin.

Now, look at the moon! How full and clear has she risen on the Racoon hunters! Now is the time for sport! Onward we go, one following the long shadow of his precursor. The twigs are no impediment, and we move at a brisker pace, as we return to the hills. What a hue and cry!—here are the dogs. Overhead and all around, on the forks of each tree, the hunter's keen eye searches for something round, which is likely to prove a coiled up Racoon. There's one! Between me and the moon I spied the cunning thing crouched in silence. After taking aim, I raise my barrel ever so little, the trigger is pressed; down falls the Racoon to the ground. Another and another are on the same tree. Off goes a bullet, then a second; and we secure the prey. "Let us go home, stranger," says the woodsman; and contented with our sport, towards his cabin we trudge. On arriving there, we find a cheerful fire. Toby stays without, prepares the game, stretches the skins on a frame of cane, and washes the bodies. The table is already set; the cake and the potatoes are all well done; four bowls of butter-milk are ranged in order; and now the hunters fall to.

The Racoon is a cunning animal, and makes a pleasant pet. Monkey-like, it is quite dexterous in the use of its fore feet, and it will amble after its master, in the manner of a bear, and even follow him into the street. It is fond of eggs, but prefers them raw, and it matters not whether it be morning, noon, or night, when it finds a dozen in the pheasant's nest, or one placed in your pocket to please him. He knows the habits of mussels better than most conchologists. Being an expert climber, he ascends to the hole of the woodpecker, and devours the young birds. He knows, too, how to watch the soft-shelled turtle's crawl, and, better still, how to dig up her eggs. Now by the edge of the pond, grimalkin-like, he lies seemingly asleep, until the summer-duck comes within reach. No Negro knows better when the corn is juicy and pleasant to eat; and although squirrels and woodpeckers know this too, the Racoon is found in the cornfield longer in the season than any of them, the havoc he commits there amounting to a tithe. His fur is good in winter, and many think his flesh good also; but for my part I prefer a live Racoon to a dead one, and should find more pleasure in hunting one than in eating him.

TRAPPING an ALLIGATOR

RALPH and CHANDOS TEMPLE

It is not uncommon for primitive, unschooled natives to put their so-called civilized betters to shame in dealing with their natural environment. Such is the case in this exciting true story of capturing the alligator-like cayman of South America alive. When more sophisticated techniques fail, an Indian comes up with a simple method that works. The account by Ralph and Chandos Temple is taken from Library of Universal Adventure *(1888), edited by William Dean Howells.*

Perhaps the most exciting of all the narratives in Mr. Waterton's travels is that which describes his efforts to entrap a cayman, and his final encounter with one of those terrible animals of the alligator kind which infest the rivers of South America. The back of the cayman is said to be almost impenetrable to a musket-ball, though his sides are not near so strong, and are easily pierced with an arrow. It is believed that no animal in existence bears more decided marks in his countenance of cruelty and malice. He is the scourge and terror of all the large rivers in South America near the line. Mr. Waterton had long desired to catch one of these monsters, and at length favorable opportunities appeared to present themselves during his third journey along the wild and solitary banks of the Essequibo. The scenes which ensue we will describe as closely as possible in the words of the adventurous naturalist. One day, an hour before sunset, he reached the place which two men, who had joined his party at the falls, had pointed out as a proper one to find a cayman. There was a large creek close by, and a sandbank gently sloping to the water. Just within the forest on this bank they cleared a piece of brushwood, suspended the hammocks from the trees, and then picked up enough of decayed wood for fuel.

They now baited a shark-hook with a large fish, and put it

upon a board, which they had brought on purpose. This board was carried out in the canoe, about forty yards into the river. By means of a string, long enough to reach the bottom of the river, and at the end of which string was fastened a stone, the board was kept, as it were, at anchor. One end of a new rope was reeved through the chain of the shark-hook, and the other end fastened to a tree on the sandbank.

It was now an hour after sunset. The sky was cloudless, and the moon shone brightly. There was not a breath of wind in the heavens, and the river seemed like a large plain of quicksilver. Every now and then a huge fish would strike and plunge in the water; then the owls and goatsuckers would continue their lamentations, and the sound of these was lost in the prowling tiger's growl. Then all was still again, and silent as midnight.

The caymen were now upon the stir, and at intervals their noise could be distinguished amid that of the jaguar, the owls, the goatsuckers, and frogs. It was a singular and awful sound, like a suppressed sigh, bursting forth all of a sudden, and so loud that you might hear it above a mile off. First one emitted this horrible noise, and then another answered him; and, on looking at the countenances of the people round him, Mr. Waterton could plainly see that they expected to have a cayman that night. The party were at supper, when the Indian said he saw the cayman coming. Upon looking towards the place there appeared something on the water like a black log of wood. It was so unlike anything alive that the Englishman doubted if it were a cayman; but the Indian smiled, and said he was sure it was one, for he remembered seeing a cayman some years ago, when he was in the Essequibo.

At last it gradually approached the bait, and the board began to move. The moon shone so bright that they could distinctly see him open his huge jaws, and take in the bait. They pulled the rope. He immediately let drop the bait, and then they saw his black head retreating from the board to the distance of a few yards, where it remained quite motionless. The monster did not seem inclined to advance again, and so they finished their supper. In about an hour's time he again put himself in motion and took hold of the bait, but did not swallow it. They pulled the rope again, but with no better success than the first time. He retreated as usual, and came back in about an hour. Thus the party watched till three o'clock in the morning, when, worn out with disappointment, they went to the hammocks, turned in, and fell asleep. When day broke they found that he had contrived to get the bait from the hook, though they had tied it on with string. They had now no more hopes of taking a cayman till the return of night. The Indian went into the woods and brought back a noble supply of game. The rest of the party went into the canoe and proceeded up the river to shoot fish, where they got even more than they could use.

The second night's attempt upon the cayman was a repetition of the first, and was quite unsuccessful. They went fishing the day after, and returned to experience a third night's disappointment. On the fourth day, about four o'clock, they began to erect a stage among the trees, close to the water's edge. From this they intended to shoot an arrow into the cayman. At the end of this arrow was to be attached a string, which would be tied to the rope; and as soon as the cayman was struck they were to have the canoe ready, and pursue him in the river.

They spent best part of the fourth night in trying for the cayman, but all to no purpose. Waterton was now convinced that something was materially wrong. He showed one of the Indians the shark-hook, who shook his head, and laughed at it, and said it would not do. When he was a boy he had seen his father catch the cayman, and on the morrow he would make something that would answer.

In the meantime they set the shark-hook, but it availed nothing; a cayman came and took it, but would not swallow it. Seeing it was useless to attend the shark-hook any longer, they left it for the night and returned to their hammocks. Ere the English naturalist fell asleep a new idea broke upon him. He considered that as far as the judgment of civilized man went, everything had been procured and done to insure success. They had hooks and lines and baits and patience, they had spent nights in watching, had seen the cayman come and take the bait, yet all had ended in disappointment.

Probably (he thought) this poor wild man of the woods would succeed by means of a very simple process; and thus prove to his more civilized brother that notwithstanding books and schools, there is a vast deal of knowledge to be picked up at every step.

In the morning, as usual, they found the bait gone from the shark-hook. The Indians went into the forest to hunt, the white men took the canoe to shoot fish and get another supply of turtles' eggs, which they found in great abundance. They then went to the little shallow creek, and shot some young caymen about two feet long. When the arrow struck them, tiny as they were, they turned round and bit it, and snapped at the men when they went into the water to take them up.

The day was now declining apace, and the Indian had made his instrument to take the cayman. It was very simple—there were four pieces of tough, hard wood, a foot long, and about as thick as a little finger, and barbed at both ends; they were tied round the end of the rope in such a manner that if the rope be imagined to be an arrow, these four sticks would form the arrow's head; so that one end of the four united sticks answered to the point of the arrow's head, while the other end expanded at equal distances round the rope.

It was evident that if the cayman swallowed this (the other end of the rope, which was thirty yards long, being fastened to a tree) the more he pulled the faster the barbs would shut. Nearly a mile from where they had their hammocks the sandbanks were steep and abrupt, and the river very still and deep; there the Indian fixed the machine, which hung suspended a foot from the water, and the end of the rope was made fast to a stake driven well into the sand.

The Indian then took the empty shell of the land-tortoise, and gave it some heavy blows with a stick. Waterton asked him why he did that, and he replied that it was to let the caymen hear that something was going on.

Having done this, the party went back to the hammocks, not intending to visit it again till morning. During the night, the jaguars roared and grumbled in the forest, and at intervals they could hear the distant cayman. "The roaring of the jaguars," says the narrative, "was awful; but it was music to the dismal noise of these hideous and malicious reptiles."

About half-past five in the morning the Indian stole off silently to take a look at the bait. On arriving at the place he set up a tremendous shout. All now jumped out of their hammocks, and ran to him.

They found a cayman, ten feet and a half long, fast to the end of the rope. Nothing now remained to do but to get him out of the water without injuring his scales. The whole party consisted of three Indians from the creek, Mr. Waterton's Indian servant, Yan, a negro called Daddy Quashi, and a man named James, whom he was instructing in the art of preserving birds.

"I informed the Indians," continues Mr. Waterton, "that it was my intention to draw him quietly out of the water, and then secure him. They looked and stared at each other, and said, 'I might do it myself, but they would have no hand in it; the cayman would worry some of us.' On saying this, they squatted on the grass with the most perfect indifference.

"The Indians of these wilds have never been subject to the least restraint; and I knew enough of them to be aware that if I tried to force them against their will they would take themselves off, and leave me and my presents unheeded, and never return.

"Daddy Quashi was for applying to our guns, as usual, considering them our best and safest friends. I immediately offered to knock him down for his cowardice, and he shrank back, begging that I would be cautious, and not get myself worried; and apologizing for his own want of resolution. My Indian was now in conversation with the others, and they asked if I would allow them to shoot a dozen arrows into him, and thus disable him. This would have ruined all. I had come above three hundred miles on purpose to get a cayman, uninjured, and not to carry back a mutilated specimen. I rejected their proposition with firmness, and darted a disdainful eye upon the Indians.

"Daddy Quashi was again beginning to remonstrate, and I chased him on the sandbank for a quarter of a mile. He told me afterwards he thought he should have dropped down dead with fright, for he was firmly persuaded, if I had caught him, I should have bundled him in the cayman's jaws. Here then we stood, in silence, like a calm before a thunderstorm. They wanted to kill him, and I wanted to take him alive.

"I now walked up and down the sand, revolving a dozen projects in my head. The canoe was at a considerable distance, and I ordered the people to bring it round to the place where we were. The mast was eight feet long, and not much thicker than my wrist. I took it out of the canoe, and wrapped the sail round the end of it. Now it appeared clear to me, that if I went down upon one knee, and held the mast in the same position as the soldier holds his bayonet when rushing to the charge, I could force it down the cayman's throat, should he come open-mouthed at me. When this was told to the Indians they brightened up, and said they would help me to pull him out of the river.

"Daddy Quashi hung in the rear. I showed him a large Spanish knife, which I always carried in the waistband of my trousers; it spoke volumes to him, and he shrugged up his shoulders in absolute despair. The sun was just peeping over the high forests on the eastern hills, as if coming to look on, and bid us act with becoming fortitude. I placed all the people at the end of the rope, and ordered them to pull till the cayman appeared on the surface of the water; and then, should he plunge, to slacken the rope, and let him go again into the deep.

"I now took the mast of the canoe in my hand (the sail being tied round the end of the mast), and sunk down upon one knee, about four yards from the water's edge, determining to thrust it down his throat, in case he gave me an opportunity. I certainly felt somewhat uncomfortable in this situation. The people pulled the cayman to the surface; he plunged furiously as soon as he arrived in these upper regions, and immediately went below again on their slackening the rope. They pulled again, and out he came. This was an interesting moment. I kept my position firmly, with my eye fixed steadfastly on him.

"By the time the cayman was within two yards of me I saw he was in a state of fear and perturbation. I instantly dropped the mast, sprung up, and jumped on his back, turning half round as I vaulted, so that I gained my seat with my face in a right position. I immediately seized his forelegs, and, by main force, twisted them on his back; thus they served me for a bridle."

The cayman now seemed to have recovered from his surprise, and, probably fancying himself in hostile company, began to plunge furiously, and lashed the sand with his long and powerful tail. Mr. Waterton was out of reach of the strokes of it, by being near his head. He continued to plunge and strike, and made his rider's seat very uncomfortable.

The people roared out in triumph, and were so vociferous that it was some time before they heard their master tell them to pull him and his singular beast of burden farther inland. He was apprehensive the rope might break, in which case there would have been every chance of going under water with the cayman.

The people now dragged them above forty yards on the sand. "It was the first and last time," says Waterton, "I was ever on a cayman's back. Should it be asked how I managed to keep my seat, I would answer, I hunted some years with Lord Darlington's fox-hounds."

After repeated attempts to regain his liberty, the cayman gave in, and became tranquil through exhaustion. They now managed to tie up his jaws, and firmly secured his fore-feet, but they had another severe struggle for superiority before the huge monster was finally conveyed to the canoe, and then to the place where they had suspended the hammocks, where, after he was slain, the enthusiastic naturalist commenced dissecting him, thus making a valuable addition to scientific knowledge.

THE FLIGHT in the HEATHER: THE ROCKS

ROBERT LOUIS STEVENSON

—a selection from Kidnapped *(1886), by Robert Louis Stevenson.*

In the wild, the hunted are not always animals. Sometimes man hunts man. In Robert Louis Stevenson's Kidnapped, *David Balfour's uncle has him kidnapped so that he can claim his nephew's inheritance. The ship bearing David off is sunk, and he escapes by swimming to shore. After a series of adventures, David and his friend Alan are pursued through the Scottish highlands under false suspicion of murder.*

Sometimes we walked, sometimes ran; and as it drew on to morning, walked ever the less and ran the more. Though, upon its face, that country appeared to be a desert, yet there were huts and houses of the people, of which we must have passed more than twenty, hidden in quiet places of the hills. When we came to one of these, Alan would leave me in the way, and go himself and rap upon the side of the house and speak a while at the window with some sleeper awakened. This was to pass the news; which in that country, was so much of a duty that Alan must pause to attend to it even while fleeing for his life; and so well attended to by others, that in more than half of the houses where we called they had heard already of the murder. In the others, as well as I could make out (standing back at a distance and hearing a strange tongue), the news was received with more of consternation than surprise.

For all our hurry, day began to come in while we were still far from any shelter. It found us in a prodigious valley, strewn with rocks and where ran a foaming river. Wild mountains stood around it; there grew there neither grass nor trees; and I have sometimes thought since then, that it may have been the valley called Glencoe, where the massacre was in the time of King William. But for the details of our itinerary, I am all to seek; our way lying now by short cuts, now by great detours; our pace being so hurried, our time of journeying usually by night; and the names of such places as I asked and heard being in the Gaelic tongue and the more easily forgotten.

The first peep of morning, then, showed us this horrible place, and I could see Alan knit his brow.

"This is no fit place for you and me," he said. "This is a place they're bound to watch."

And with that he ran harder than ever down to the water side, in a part where the river was split in two among three rocks. It went through with a horrid thundering that made my belly quake; and there hung over the lynn* a little mist of spray. Alan looked neither to the right nor to the left, but jumped clean upon the middle rock and fell there on his hands and knees to check himself, for that rock was small and he might have pitched over on the far side. I had scarce time to measure the distance or to understand the peril before I had followed him, and he had caught and stopped me.

So there we stood, side by side upon a small rock slippery with spray, a far broader leap in front of us, and the river dinning upon all sides. When I saw where I was, there came on me a deadly sickness of fear, and I put my hand over my eyes. Alan took me and shook me; I saw he was speaking, but the roaring of the falls and the trouble of my mind prevented me from hearing; only I saw his face was red with anger, and that he stamped upon the rock. The same look showed me the water raging by, and the mist hanging in the air: and with that I covered my eyes again and shuddered.

The next minute Alan had set the brandy bottle to my lips, and forced me to drink about a gill, which sent the blood into my head again. Then, putting his hands to his mouth, and his mouth to my ear, he shouted, "Hang or drown!" and turning his back upon me, leaped over the farther branch of the stream, and landed safe.

I was now alone upon the rock, which gave me the more room; the brandy was singing in my ears; I had this good example fresh before me, and just wit enough to see that if I did not leap at

---

* waterfall

once, I should never leap at all. I bent low on my knees and flung myself forth, with that kind of anger of despair that has sometimes stood me in stead of courage. Sure enough, it was but my hands that reached the full length; these slipped, caught again, slipped again; and I was sliddering back into the lynn, when Alan seized me, first by the hair, then by the collar, and with a great strain dragged me into safety.

Never a word he said, but set off running again for his life, and I must stagger to my feet and run after him. I had been weary before, but now I was sick and bruised, and partly drunken with the brandy; I kept stumbling as I ran, I had a stitch that came near to overmaster me; and when at last Alan paused under a great rock that stood there among a number of others, it was none too soon for David Balfour.

A great rock I have said; but by rights it was two rocks leaning together at the top, both some twenty feet high, and at the first sight inaccessible. Even Alan (though you may say he had as good as four hands) failed twice in an attempt to climb them; and it was only at the third trial, and then by standing on my shoulders and leaping up with such force as I thought must have broken my collarbone, that he secured a lodgment. Once there, he let down his leathern girdle; and with the aid of that and a pair of shallow footholds in the rock, I scrambled up beside him.

Then I saw why we had come there; for the two rocks, being both somewhat hollow on the top and sloping one to the other, made a kind of dish or saucer, where as many as three or four men might have lain hidden.

All this while Alan had not said a word, and had run and climbed with such a savage, silent frenzy of hurry, that I knew that he was in mortal fear of some miscarriage. Even now we were on the rock he said nothing, nor so much as relaxed the frowning look upon his face; but clapped flat down, and keeping only one eye above the edge of our place of shelter scouted all round the compass. The dawn had come quite clear; we could see the stony sides of the valley, and its bottom, which was bestrewed with rocks, and the river, which went from one side to another, and made white falls; but nowhere the smoke of a house, nor any living creature but some eagles screaming round a cliff.

Then at last Alan smiled.

"Ay," said he, "now we have a chance"; and then looking at

me with some amusement, "Ye're no very gleg* at the jumping," said he.

At this I suppose I coloured with mortification, for he added at once, "Hoots! Small blame to ye! To be feared of a thing and yet to do it, is what makes the prettiest kind of a man. And then there was water there, and water's a thing that dauntons even me. No, no," said Alan, "it's no you that's to blame, it's me."

I asked him why.

"Why," said he, "I have proved myself a gomeral† this night. For first of all I take a wrong road, and that in my own country of Appin; so that the day has caught us where we should never have been; and thanks to that, we lie here in some danger and mair discomfort. And next (which is the worst of the two, for a man that has been so much among the heather as myself) I have come wanting a water bottle, and here we lie for a long summer's day with naething but neat spirit. Ye may think that a small matter; but before it comes night, David, ye'll give me news of it."

I was anxious to redeem my character, and offered, if he would pour out the brandy, to run down and fill the bottle at the river.

"I wouldnae waste the good spirit either," says he. "It's been a good friend to you this night; or in my poor opinion, ye would still be cocking on yon stone. And what's mair," says he, "ye may have observed (you that's a man of so much penetration) that Alan Breck Stewart was perhaps walking quicker than his ordinar'."

"You!" I cried, "you were running fit to burst."

"Was I so?" said he. "Well, then, ye may depend upon it, there was nae time to be lost. And now here is enough said; gang you to your sleep, lad, and I'll watch."

Accordingly, I lay down to sleep; a little peaty earth had drifted in between the top of the two rocks, and some bracken grew there, to be a bed to me; the last thing I heard was still the crying of the eagles.

I dare say it would be nine in the morning when I was roughly awakened, and found Alan's hand pressed upon my mouth.

"Wheesht!" he whispered. "Ye were snoring."

"Well," said I, surprised at his anxious and dark face, "and why not?"

---

*Brisk. †Fool.

He peered over the edge of the rock, and signed to me to do the like.

It was now high day, cloudless, and very hot. The valley was as clear as in a picture. About half a mile up the water was a camp of redcoats; a big fire blazed in their midst, at which some were cooking; and nearby, on the top of a rock about as high as ours, there stood a sentry, with the sun sparkling on his arms. All the way down along the riverside were posted other sentries; here near together, there widelier scattered; some planted like the first, on places of command, some on the ground level and marching and countermarching, so as to meet halfway. Higher up the glen, where the ground was more open, the chain of posts was continued by horse soldiers, whom we could see in the distance riding to and fro. Lower down, the infantry continued; but as the stream was suddenly swelled by the confluence of a considerable burn, they were more widely set, and only watched the fords and stepping-stones.

I took but one look at them, and ducked again into my place. It was strange indeed to see this valley, which had lain so solitary in the hour of dawn, bristling with arms and dotted with the red coats and breeches.

"Ye see," said Alan, "this was what I was afraid of, Davie: that they would watch the burnside. They began to come in about two hours ago, and, man! but ye're a grand hand at the sleeping! We're in a narrow place. If they get up the sides of the hill, they could easy spy us with a glass; but if they'll only keep in the foot of the valley, we'll do yet. The posts are thinner down the water; and, come night, we'll try our hand at getting by them."

"And what are we to do till night?" I asked.

"Lie here," says he, "and birstle."*

That one good Scotch word, "birstle," was indeed the most of the story of the day that we had now to pass. You are to remember that we lay on the bare top of a rock, like scones upon a girdle; the sun beat upon us cruelly; the rock grew so heated, a man could scarce endure the touch of it; and the little patch of earth and fern, which kept cooler, was only large enough for one at a time. We took turn about to lie on the naked rock, which was indeed like the position of that saint that was martyred on a gridiron; and it ran in my mind how strange it was,

---

*Toast hard.

that in the same climate and at only a few days' distance, I should have suffered so cruelly, first from cold upon my island and now from heat upon this rock.

All the while we had no water, only raw brandy for a drink, which was worse than nothing; but we kept the bottle as cool as we could, burying it in the earth, and got some relief by bathing our breasts and temples.

The soldiers kept stirring all day in the bottom of the valley, now changing guard, now in patrolling parties hunting among the rocks. These lay round in so great a number, that to look for men among them was like looking for a needle in a bottle of hay; and being so hopeless a task, it was gone about with the less care. Yet we could see the soldiers pike their bayonets among the heather, which sent a cold thrill into my vitals; and they would sometimes hang about our rock, so that we scarce dared to breathe.

It was in this way that I first heard the right English speech; one fellow as he went by actually clapping his hand upon the sunny face of the rock on which we lay, and plucking it off again with an oath. "I tell you it's 'ot," says he; and I was amazed at the clipping tones and the odd singsong in which he spoke, and no less at that strange trick of dropping out the letter "h." To be sure, I had heard Ransome; but he had taken his ways from all sorts of people, and spoke so imperfectly at the best, that I set down the most of it to childishness. My surprise was all the greater to hear that manner of speaking in the mouth of a grown man; and indeed I have never grown used to it; nor yet altogether with the English grammar, as perhaps a very critical eye might here and there spy out even in these memoirs.

The tediousness and pain of these hours upon the rock grew only the greater as the day went on; the rock getting still the hotter and the sun fiercer. There were giddiness, and sickness, and sharp pangs like rheumatism, to be supported. I minded then, and have often minded since, on the lines in our Scotch psalm:—

The moon by night thee shall not smite,
Nor yet the sun by day;

and indeed it was only by God's blessing that we were neither of us sun-smitten.

At last, about two, it was beyond men's bearing, and there

was now temptation to resist, as well as pain to thole.* For the sun being now got a little into the west, there came a patch of shade on the east side of our rock, which was the side sheltered from the soldiers.

"As well one death as another," said Alan, and slipped over the edge and dropped on the ground on the shadowy side.

I followed him at once, and instantly fell all my length, so weak was I and so giddy with that long exposure. Here, then, we lay for an hour or two, aching from head to foot, as weak as water, and lying quite naked to the eye of any soldier who should have strolled that way. None came, however, all passing by on the other side; so that our rock continued to be our shield even in this new position.

Presently we began again to get a little strength; and as the soldiers were now lying closer along the riverside, Alan proposed that we should try a start. I was by this time afraid of but one thing in the world; and that was to be set back upon the rock; anything else was welcome to me; so we got ourselves at once in marching order, and began to slip from rock to rock one after the other, now crawling flat on our bellies in the shade, now making a run for it, heart in mouth.

The soldiers, having searched this side of the valley after a fashion, and being perhaps somewhat sleepy with the sultriness of the afternoon, had now laid by much of their vigilance, and stood dozing at their posts or only kept a lookout along the banks of the river; so that in this way, keeping down the valley and at the same time towards the mountains, we drew steadily away from their neighbourhood. But the business was the most wearing I had ever taken part in. A man had need of a hundred eyes in every part of him, to keep concealed in that uneven country and within cry of so many and scattered sentries. When we must pass an open place, quickness was not all, but a swift judgment not only of the lie of the whole country, but of the solidity of every stone on which we must set foot; for the afternoon was now fallen so breathless that the rolling of a pebble sounded abroad like a pistol shot, and would start the echo calling among the hills and cliffs.

By sundown we had made some distance, even by our slow rate of progress, though to be sure the sentry on the rock was

*Suffer.

still plainly in our view. But now we came on something that put all fears out of season; and that was a deep rushing burn, that tore down, in that part, to join the glen river. At the sight of this we cast ourselves on the ground and plunged head and shoulders in the water; and I cannot tell which was the more pleasant, the great shock as the cool stream went over us, or the greed with which we drank of it.

We lay there (for the banks hid us), drank again and again, bathed our chests, let our wrists trail in the running water till they ached with the chill; and at last, being wonderfully renewed, we got out the meal bag and made drammach in the iron pan. This, though it is but cold water mingled with oatmeal, yet makes a good enough dish for a hungry man; and where there are no means of making fire, or (as in our case) good reason for not making one, it is the chief stand-by of those who have taken to the heather.

As soon as the shadow of the night had fallen, we set forth again, at first with the same caution, but presently with more boldness, standing our full height and stepping out at a good pace of walking. The way was very intricate, lying up the steep sides of mountains and along the brows of cliffs; clouds had come in with the sunset, and the night was dark and cool; so that I walked without much fatigue, but in continual fear of falling and rolling down the mountains, and with no guess at our direction.

The moon rose at last and found us still on the road; it was in its last quarter, and was long beset with clouds; but after a while shone out and showed me many dark heads of mountains, and was reflected far underneath us on the narrow arm of a sea-loch.

At this sight we both paused: I struck with wonder to find myself so high and walking (as it seemed to me) upon clouds; Alan to make sure of his direction.

Seemingly he was well pleased, and he must certainly have judged us out of earshot of all our enemies; for throughout the rest of our night march he beguiled the way with whistling of many tunes, warlike, merry, plaintive; reel tunes that made the foot go faster; tunes of my own south country that made me fain to be home from my adventures; and all these, on the great, dark desert mountains, making company upon the way.

AN UNCANNY TALE

THEODORE ROOSEVELT

—a selection from Ranch Life and the Hunting-Trail *(1888), by Theodore Roosevelt.*

Much of the North Dakota badlands, where Theodore Roosevelt ranched in his youth, is now the Theodore Roosevelt National Memorial Park. In the nineteenth century when Roosevelt lived there, it was still the "Wild West." In his books he later described the frontier types he met and some of the tall stories they told.

On one of my trips to the mountains, I happened to come across several old-style hunters at the same time. Two were on their way out of the woods, after having been all winter and spring without seeing a white face. They had been lucky, and their battered packsaddles carried bales of valuable furs—fisher, sable, otter, mink, beaver. The two men, though fast friends and allies for many years, contrasted oddly. One was a short, square-built, good-humored Kanuck, always laughing and talking, who interlarded his conversation with a singularly original mixture of the most villainous French and English profanity. His partner was an American, gray-eyed, tall and straight as a young pine, with a saturnine, rather haughty face, and proud bearing. He spoke very little, and then in low tones, never using an oath; but he showed now and then a most unexpected sense of dry humor. Both were images of bronzed and rugged strength. Neither had the slightest touch of the bully in his nature; they treated others with the respect that they also exacted for themselves. They bore an excellent reputation as being not only highly skilled in woodcraft and the use of the rifle, but also men of tried courage and strict integrity whose word could be always implicitly trusted.

I had with me at the time a hunter who, though their equal as marksman or woodsman, was their exact opposite morally. He was a pleasant companion and useful assistant, being very hard working and possessing a temper that never was ruffled by anything. He was also a good-looking fellow, with honest brown eyes; but he no more knew the difference between right and wrong than Adam did before the fall. Had he been at all conscious of his wickedness, or had he possessed the least sense of shame, he would have been unbearable as a companion; but he was so perfectly pleasant and easy, so good-humoredly tolerant of virtue in others, and he so wholly lacked even a glimmering suspicion that murder, theft, and adultery were matters of anything more than individual taste, that I actually grew to be rather fond of him. He never related any of his past deeds of wickedness as matters either for boastfulness or for regret; they were simply repeated incidentally in the course of conversation. Thus, once in speaking of the profits of his different enterprises, he casually mentioned making a good deal of money as a government scout in the Southwest by buying cartridges from some Negro troops at a cent apiece and selling them to the hostile Apaches for a dollar each. His conduct was not due to sympathy with the Indians, for it appeared that later on he had taken part in massacring some of these same Apaches when they were prisoners. He brushed aside as irrelevant one or two questions which I put to him; matters of sentiment were not to be mixed up with a purely mercantile speculation. Another time we were talking of the curious angles bullets sometimes fly off at when they ricochet. To illustrate the matter he related an experience which I shall try to give in his own words. "One time, when I was keeping a saloon down in New Mexico, there was a man owed me a grudge. Well, he took sick of the smallpox, and the doctor told him he'd sure die, and he said if that was so he reckoned he'd kill me first. So he come a-riding in with his gun [in the West a revolver is generally called a gun] and begun shooting; but I hit him first, and away he rode. I started to get on my horse to follow him; but there was a little Irishman there who said he'd never killed a man, and he begged hard for me to give him my gun and let him go after the other man and finish him. So I let him go; and when he caught up, blamed if the little cuss didn't get so nervous that he fired off into the ground, and the darned bullet struck a crow-bar, and glanced up, and hit the other man square in the head and killed him! Now, that *was* a funny shot, wasn't it?"

The fourth member of our party round the campfire that night was a powerfully built trapper, partly French by blood, who wore a gaily colored capote, or blanket-coat, a greasy fur cap, and moccasins. He had grizzled hair, and a certain uneasy, half-furtive look about the eyes. Once or twice he showed a curious reluctance about allowing a man to approach him suddenly from behind. Altogether his actions were so odd that I felt some curiosity to learn his history. It turned out that he had been through a rather uncanny experience the winter before. He and another man had gone into a remote basin, or enclosed valley, in the heart of the mountains, where game was very plentiful; indeed, it was so abundant that they decided to pass the winter there. Accordingly they put up a log cabin, working hard, and merely killing enough meat for their immediate use. Just as it was finished winter set in with tremendous snow-storms. Going out to hunt, in the first lull, they found, to their consternation, that every head of game had left the valley. Not an animal was to be found therein; they had abandoned it for their winter haunts. The outlook for the two adventurers was appalling. They were afraid of trying to break out through the deep snowdrifts, and starvation stared them in the face if they stayed. The man I met had his dog with him. They put themselves on very short commons, so as to use up their flour as slowly as possible, and hunted unweariedly, but saw nothing. Soon a violent quarrel broke out between them. The other man, a fierce, sullen fellow, insisted that the dog should be killed, but the owner was exceedingly attached to it and refused. For a couple of weeks they spoke no word to each other, though cooped in the little narrow pen of logs. Then one night the owner of the dog was wakened by the animal crying out; the other man had tried to kill it with his knife, but failed. The provisions were now almost exhausted, and the two men were glaring at each other with the rage of maddened, ravening hunger. Neither dared to sleep, for fear that the other would kill him. Then the one who owned the dog at last spoke, and proposed that, to give each a chance for his life, they should separate. He would take half of the handful of flour that was left and start off to try to get home; the other should stay where he was; and if he tried to follow the first, he was warned that he would be shot without mercy. A like fate was to be the portion of the wanderer if driven to return to the hut. The arrangement was agreed to and the two men separated, neither daring to turn his back while they were within rifle-shot of each other. For two days the one who went off toiled on with weary weakness through the snowdrifts. Late on the second afternoon, as he looked back from a high ridge, he saw in the far distance a black speck against the snow, coming along on his trail. His companion was dogging his footsteps. Immediately he followed his own trail back a little and lay in ambush. At dusk his companion came stealthily up, rifle in hand, peering cautiously ahead, his drawn face showing the starved, eager ferocity of a wild beast, and the man he was hunting shot him down exactly as if he had been one. Leaving the body where it fell, the wanderer continued his journey, the dog staggering painfully behind him. The next evening he baked his last cake and divided it with the dog. In the morning, with his belt drawn still tighter round his skeleton body, he once more set out, with apparently only a few hours of dull misery between him and death. At noon he crossed the track of a huge timber wolf; instantly the dog gave tongue, and rallying its strength, ran along the trail. The man struggled after. At last his strength gave out and he sat down to die; but while sitting still, slowly stiffening with the cold, he heard the dog baying in the woods. Shaking off his mortal numbness, he crawled toward the sound, and found the wolf over the body of a deer that he had just killed, and keeping the dog from it. At the approach of the new assailant the wolf sullenly drew off, and man and dog tore the raw deer-flesh with hideous eagerness. It made them very sick for the next twenty-four hours; but, lying by the carcass for two or three days, they recovered strength. A week afterward the trapper reached a miner's cabin in safety. There he told his tale, and the unknown man who alone might possibly have contradicted it lay dead in the depths of the wolf-haunted forest.

PART V

The Perennial Source of Our Life

SERMONS in STONES

WILLIAM SHAKESPEARE

—a selection from As You Like It *(1599-1600), by William Shakespeare.*

Shakespeare used outdoor backgrounds for many of his plays, notably, The Tempest, A Midsummer Night's Dream, *and* As You Like It, *where most of the action takes place in the Forest of Arden. The Duke, who has been banished there, points out the advantages of life in the wild to his followers in a famous speech (Act II, scene i, ll. 2-17).*

Hath not old custom made this life more sweet
Than that of painted pomp? Are not these woods
More free from peril than the envious court?
Here feel we but the penalty of Adam,
The seasons' difference; as the icy fang
And churlish chiding of the winter's wind,
Which, when it bites and blows upon my body,
Even till I shrink with cold, I smile and say
"This is no flattery: these are counsellors
That feelingly persuade me what I am."
Sweet are the uses of adversity;
Which, like the toad, ugly and venomous,
Wears yet a precious jewel in his head:
And this our life exempt from public haunt
Finds tongues in trees, books in running brooks,
Sermons in stones and good in every thing.

SELECTIONS from WALDEN

HENRY DAVID THOREAU

Henry David Thoreau was a man who really "got away from it all." He realized that many men, rather than owning possessions, were possessed by them, and he set out to prove how very little was needed for human happiness. In 1854, he wrote Walden, *as an autobiography of two years of self-sufficient life at Walden Pond in Massachusetts.*

The first excerpt below, entitled "Solitude" by Thoreau, reveals the inspiration which the writer found in the quiet of the wilderness, where there is no loneliness for the person who is at one with God's universe.

The second, which the author called "Winter Animals," is quite similar in mood to the first. It describes the delights of winter—the unfamiliar perspectives afforded by walking over frozen ponds and the wild, wonderful sounds of owls, geese, foxes, and whooping pond ice heard during winter nights.

This is a delicious evening, when the whole body is one sense, and imbibes delight through every pore. I go and come with a strange liberty in Nature, a part of herself. As I walk along the stony shore of the pond in my shirt-sleeves, though it is cool as well as cloudy and windy, and I see nothing special to attract me, all the elements are unusually congenial to me. The bullfrogs trump to usher in the night, and the note of the whip-poor-will is borne on the rippling wind from over the water. Sympathy with the fluttering alder and poplar leaves almost takes away my breath; yet, like the lake, my serenity is rippled but not ruffled. These small waves raised by the evening wind are as remote from storm as the smooth reflecting surface. Though it is now dark, the wind still blows and roars in the wood, the waves still dash, and some creatures lull the rest with their notes. The repose is never complete. The wildest animals do not repose, but seek their prey now; the fox, and skunk, and rabbit, now roam the fields and woods without fear. They are Nature's watchmen—links which connect the days of animated life.

When I return to my house I find that visitors have been there and left their cards, either a bunch of flowers, or a wreath of evergreen, or a name in pencil on a yellow walnut leaf or a chip. They who come rarely to the woods take some little piece of the forest into their hands to play with by the way, which they leave, either intentionally or accidentally. One has peeled a willow wand, woven it into a ring, and dropped it on my table. I could always tell if visitors had called in my absence, either by the bended twigs or grass, or the print of their shoes, and generally of what sex or age or quality they were by some slight trace left, as a flower dropped, or a bunch of grass plucked and thrown away, even as far off as the railroad, half a mile distant, or by the lingering odor of a cigar or pipe. . . .

There is commonly sufficient space about us. Our horizon is never quite at our elbows. The thick wood is not just at our door, nor the pond, but somewhat is always clearing, familiar and worn by us, appropriated and fenced in some way, and reclaimed from Nature. For what reason have I this vast range and circuit, some square miles of unfrequented forest, for my privacy, abandoned to me by men? My nearest neighbor is a mile distant, and no house is visible from any place but the hill-tops within half a mile of my own. I have my horizon bounded by woods all to myself; a distant view of the railroad where it touches the pond on the one hand, and of the fence which skirts the woodland road on the other. But for the most part it is as solitary where I live as on the prairies. It is as much Asia or Africa as New England. I have, as it were, my own sun and moon and stars, and a little world all to myself. At night there was never a traveller passed my house, or knocked at my door, more than if I were the first or last man; unless it were in the spring, when at long intervals some came from the village to fish for pouts,—they plainly fished much more in Walden Pond of their own natures, and baited their hooks with darkness—but they soon retreated, usually with light baskets, and left "the world to darkness and to me," and the black kernel of the night was never profaned by any human neighborhood. . . .

Yet I experienced sometimes that the most sweet and tender, the most innocent and encouraging society may be found in any natural object, even for the poor misanthrope and most melancholy man. There can be no very black melancholy to him who lives in the midst of nature and has his senses still. There was never yet such a storm but it was Aeolian music to a healthy and innocent ear. Nothing can rightly compel a simple and brave man to a vulgar sadness. While I enjoy the friendship of the seasons I trust that nothing can make life a burden to me. The gentle rain which waters my beans and keeps me in the house today is not drear and melancholy, but good for me too. Though it prevents my hoeing them, it is of far more worth than my hoeing. If it should continue so long as to cause the seeds to rot in the ground and destroy the potatoes in the low lands, it would still be good for the grass on the uplands, and, being good for the grass, it would be good for me. Sometimes, when I compare myself with other men, it seems as if I were more favored by the gods than they, beyond any deserts that I am conscious of; as if I had a warrant and surety at their hands which my fellows have not, and were especially guided and guarded. I do not flatter myself, but if it be possible they flatter me. I have never felt lonesome, or in the least oppressed by a sense of solitude, but once, and that was a few weeks after I came to the woods, when, for an hour, I doubted if the near neighborhood of man was not essential to a serene and healthy life. To be alone was something unpleasant. But I was at the same time conscious of a slight insanity in my mood, and seemed to foresee my recovery. In the midst of a gentle rain while these thoughts prevailed, I was suddenly sensible of such sweet and beneficent society in Nature, in the very pattering of the drops, and in every sound and sight around my house, an infinite and unaccountable friendliness all at once like an atmosphere sustaining me, as made the fancied advantages of human neighborhood insignificant, and I have never thought of them since. Every little pine needle expanded and swelled with sympathy and befriended me. I was so distinctly made aware of the presence of something kindred to me, even in scenes which we are accustomed to call wild and dreary, and also that the nearest of blood to me and humanest was not a person nor a villager, that I thought no place could be strange to me again. . . .

Some of my pleasantest hours were during the long rainstorms in the spring or fall, which confined me to the house for the afternoon as well as the forenoon, soothed by their ceaseless roar and pelting; when an early twilight ushered in a long evening in which many thoughts had time to take root and unfold themselves. In those driving northeast rains which tried the village houses so, when the maids stood ready with mop and pail in front entries to keep the deluge out, I sat behind my door in my little house, which was all entry, and thoroughly enjoyed its protection. In one heavy thunder-shower the lightning struck a large pitch pine across the pond, making a very conspicuous and perfectly regular spiral groove from top to bottom, an inch or more deep, and four or five inches wide, as you would groove a walking-stick. I passed it again the other day, and was struck with awe on looking up and beholding that mark, now more distinct than ever, where a terrific and resistless bolt came down out of the harmless sky eight years ago. Men frequently say to me, "I should think you would feel lonesome down there, and want to be nearer to folks, rainy and snowy days and nights especially." I am tempted to reply to such,—This whole earth which we inhabit is but a point in space. How far apart, think you, dwell the two most distant inhabitants of yonder star, the breadth of whose disk cannot be appreciated by our instruments? Why should I feel lonely? is not our planet in the Milky Way? . . .

I have heard of a man lost in the woods and dying of famine and exhaustion at the foot of a tree, whose loneliness was relieved by the grotesque visions with which, owing to bodily weakness, his diseased imagination surrounded him, and which he believed to be real. So also, owing to bodily health and strength, we may be continually cheered by a like but more normal and natural society, and come to know that we are never alone.

I have a great deal of company in my house; especially in the morning, when nobody calls. Let me suggest a few comparisons, that some one may convey an idea of my situation. I am no more lonely than the loon in the pond that laughs so loud, or than Walden Pond itself. What company has that lonely lake, I pray? And yet it has not the blue devils, but the blue angels in it, in the azure tint of its waters. The sun is alone, except in thick weather, when there sometimes appear to be two, but one is a mock sun. God is alone,—but the devil, he is far from being alone; he sees a great deal of company; he is legion. I am no more lonely than a single mullein or dandelion in a pasture, or a bean leaf, or sorrel, or a horse-fly, or a bumblebee. I am no more lonely than the Mill Brook, or a weathercock, or the north star. . . .

* * * * * * * * * * * * * * * *

When the ponds were firmly frozen, they afforded not only new and shorter routes to many points, but new views from their surfaces of the familiar landscape around them. When I crossed Flint's Pond, after it was covered with snow, though I had often paddled about and skated over it, it was so unexpectedly wide and so strange that I could think of nothing but Baffin's Bay. The Lincoln hills rose up around me at the extremity of a snowy plain, in which I did not remember to have stood before; and the fishermen, at an indeterminable distance over the ice, moving slowly about with their wolfish dogs, passed for sealers or Esquimaux, or in misty weather loomed like fabulous creatures, and I did not know whether they were giants or pygmies. I took this course when I went to lecture in Lincoln in the evening, travelling in no road and passing no house between my own hut and the lecture room. In Goose Pond, which lay in my way, a colony of muskrats dwelt, and raised their cabins high above the ice, though none could be seen abroad when I crossed it. Walden, being like the rest usually bare of snow, or with only shallow and interrupted drifts on it, was my yard where I could walk freely when the snow was nearly two feet deep on a level elsewhere and the villagers were confined to their streets. There, far from the village street, and except at very long intervals, from the jingle of sleigh-bells, I slid and skated, as in a vast moose-yard well trodden, overhung by oak woods and solemn pines bent down with snow or bristling with icicles.

For sounds in winter nights, and often in winter days, I heard the forlorn but melodious note of a hooting owl indefinitely far; such a sound as the frozen earth would yield if struck with a suitable plectrum, the very *lingua vernacula* of Walden Wood, and quite familiar to me at last, though I never saw the bird while it was making it. I seldom opened my door in a winter evening without hearing it; *Hoo hoo hoo, hoorer hoo*, sounded sonorously, and the first three syllables accented somewhat like *how der do;* or sometimes *hoo hoo* only. One night in the beginning of winter, before the pond froze over, about nine o'clock, I was startled by the loud honking of a goose, and, stepping to the door, heard the sound of their wings like a tempest in the woods as they flew low over my house. They passed over the pond toward Fair Haven, seemingly deterred from settling by my light, their commodore honking all the while with a regular beat. Suddenly an unmistakable cat owl from very near me, with the most harsh and tremendous voice I ever heard from any inhabitant of the woods, responded at regular intervals to the goose, as if determined to expose and disgrace this intruder from Hudson's Bay by exhibiting a greater compass and volume of voice in a native, and *boo-hoo* him out of Concord horizon. What do you mean by alarming the citadel at this time of night consecrated to me? Do you think I am ever caught napping at such an hour, and that I have not got lungs and a larynx as well as yourself? *Boo-hoo, boo-hoo, boo-hoo!* It was one of the most thrilling discords I ever heard. And yet, if you had a discriminating ear, there were in it the elements of a concord such as these plains never saw nor heard.

I also heard the whooping of the ice in the pond, my great bedfellow in that part of Concord, as if it were restless in its bed and would fain turn over, were troubled with flatulency and bad dreams; or I was waked by the cracking of the ground by the frost, as if some one had driven a team against my door, and in the morning would find a crack in the earth a quarter of a mile long and a third of an inch wide.

Sometimes I heard the foxes as they ranged over the snow-crusts, in moonlight nights, in search of a partridge or other game, barking raggedly and demoniacally like forest dogs, as if laboring with some anxiety, or seeking expression, struggling for light and to be dogs outright and run freely in the streets. . . .

LAKE TAHOE

MARK TWAIN

—a selection from Roughing It *(1872), by Mark Twain. Samuel Clemens (better known as Mark Twain) and a friend visited Lake Tahoe before it became a fashionable resort. Later, he wrote the following account of his trip—a paean to the medicinal, restorative properties of the beautiful lake.*

It was the end of August, and the skies were cloudless and the weather superb. In two or three weeks I had grown wonderfully fascinated with the curious new country, and concluded to put off my return to "the States" awhile. I had grown well accustomed to wearing a damaged slouch hat, blue woolen shirt, and pants crammed into boot-tops, and gloried in the absence of coat, vest, and braces. I felt rowdyish and "bully," (as the historian Josephus phrases it, in his fine chapter upon the destruction of the Temple). It seemed to me that nothing could be so fine and so romantic. I had become an officer of the government, but that was for mere sublimity. The office was an unique sinecure. I had nothing to do and no salary. I was private secretary to his majesty the Secretary, and there was not yet writing enough for two of us. So Johnny K—— and I devoted our time to amusement. He was the young son of an Ohio nabob and was out there for recreation. He got it. We had heard a world of talk about the marvelous beauty of Lake Tahoe, and finally curiosity drove us thither to see it. Three or four members of the Brigade had been there and located some timber lands on its shores and stored up a quantity of provisions in their camp. We strapped a couple of blankets on our shoulders and took an axe apiece and started—for we intended to take up a wood ranch or so ourselves and become wealthy. We were on foot. The reader will find it advantageous to go horseback. We were told that the distance was eleven miles. We tramped a long time on level ground, and then toiled laboriously up a mountain about a thousand miles high and looked over. No lake there. We descended on the other side, crossed the valley and toiled up another mountain three or four thousand miles high, apparently, and looked over again. No lake yet. We sat down tired and perspiring, and hired a couple of Chinamen to curse those people who had beguiled us. Thus refreshed, we presently resumed the march with renewed vigor and determination. We plodded on, two or three hours longer, and at last the Lake burst upon us—a noble sheet of blue water lifted six thousand three hundred feet above the level of the sea, and walled in by a rim of snow-clad mountain peaks that towered aloft full three thousand feet higher still! It was a vast oval, and one would have to use up eighty or a hundred good miles in traveling around it. As it lay there with the shadows of the mountains brilliantly photographed upon its still surface I thought it must surely be the fairest picture the whole earth affords.

We found the small skiff belonging to the Brigade boys, and without loss of time set out across a deep bend of the lake toward the landmarks that signified the locality of the camp. I got Johnny to row—not because I mind exertion myself, but because it makes me sick to ride backwards when I am at work. But I steered. A three-mile pull brought us to the camp just as the night fell, and we stepped ashore very tired and wolfishly hungry. In a "cache" among the rocks we found the provisions and the cooking utensils, and then, all fatigued as I was, I sat down on a boulder and superintended while Johnny gathered wood and cooked supper. Many a man who had gone through what I had, would have wanted to rest.

It was a delicious supper—hot bread, fried bacon, and black coffee. It was a delicious solitude we were in, too. Three miles away was a saw-mill and some workmen, but there were not fifteen other human beings throughout the wide circumference of the lake. As the darkness closed down and the stars came out and spangled the great mirror with jewels, we smoked meditatively in the solemn hush and forgot our troubles and our pains. In due time we spread our blankets in the warm sand between two large boulders and soon fell asleep, careless of the procession of ants that passed in through rents in our clothing and explored our persons. Nothing could disturb the sleep that fettered us, for it had been fairly earned, and if our consciences had any sins on them they had to adjourn court for that night, any way. The wind rose just as we were losing consciousness, and we were lulled to sleep by the beating of the surf upon the shore.

It is always very cold on that lake shore in the night, but we had plenty of blankets and were warm enough. We never moved a muscle all night, but waked at early dawn in the original positions, and got up at once, thoroughly refreshed, free from soreness, and brim full of friskiness. There is no end of wholesome medicine in such an experience. That morning we could have whipped ten such people as we were the day before—sick ones at any rate. But the world is slow, and people will go to "water cures" and "movement cures" and to foreign lands for health. Three months of camp life on Lake Tahoe would restore an Egyptian mummy to his pristine vigor, and give him an appetite like an alligator. I do not mean the oldest and driest mummies, of course, but the fresher ones. The air up there in the clouds is very pure and fine, bracing and delicious. And why shouldn't it be?—it is the same the angels breathe. . . .

BEAUTY

RALPH WALDO EMERSON

—a selection from Nature *(1836), by Ralph Waldo Emerson.*
Ralph Waldo Emerson was indeed a versatile man whose talents were too broad to fit into any conventional niche. He was educated for the Unitarian ministry, but retired from the pastorate of the Old North Church, Boston, because of doctrinal difficulties. As a lecturer and philosopher, he became known as one of the foremost exponents of transcendentalism, together with his friend Thoreau. Emerson's essays and poetry reveal the great inspiration he found in the outdoors. His essay, "Beauty," is an outstanding example of his reaction to the loveliness of nature.

A nobler want of man is served by nature, namely, the love of Beauty.

The ancient Greeks called the world κόσμος, beauty. Such is the constitution of all things, or such the plastic power of the human eye, that the primary forms, as the sky, the mountain, the tree, the animal, give us a delight *in and for themselves;* a pleasure arising from outline, color, motion, and grouping. This seems partly owing to the eye itself. The eye is the best of artists. By the mutual action of its structure and of the laws of light, perspective is produced, which integrates every mass of objects, of what character soever, into a well colored and shaded globe, so that where the particular objects are mean and unaffecting, the landscape which they compose is round and symmetrical. And as the eye is the best composer, so light is the first of painters. There is no object so foul that intense light will not make beautiful. And the stimulus it affords to the sense, and a sort of infinitude which it hath, like space and time, make all matter gay. Even the corpse has its own beauty. But besides this general grace diffused over nature, almost all the individual forms are agreeable to the eye, as is proved by our endless imitations of some of them, as the acorn, the grape, the pine-cone, the wheat-ear, the egg, the wings and forms of most birds, the lion's claw, the serpent, the butterfly, sea-shells, flames, clouds, buds, leaves, and the forms of many trees, as the palm.

For better consideration, we may distribute the aspects of Beauty in a threefold manner.

1. First, the simple perception of natural forms is a delight. The influence of the forms and actions in nature is so needful to man, that, in its lowest functions, it seems to lie on the confines of commodity and beauty. To the body and mind which have been cramped by noxious work or company, nature is medicinal and restores their tone. The tradesman, the attorney, comes out of the din and craft of the street and sees the sky and the woods, and is a man again. In their eternal calm, he finds himself. The health of the eye seems to demand a horizon. We are never tired, so long as we can see far enough.

But in other hours, Nature satisfies by its loveliness, and without any mixture of corporeal benefit. I see the spectacle of morning from the hilltop over against my house, from daybreak to sunrise with emotions which an angel might share. The long slender bars of cloud float like fishes in the sea of crimson light. From the earth, as a shore, I look out into that silent sea. I seem to partake its rapid transformations; the active enchantment reaches my dust, and I dilate and conspire with the morning wind. How does Nature deify us with a few and cheap elements! Give me health and a day, and I will make the pomp of emperors ridiculous. The dawn is my Assyria; the sunset and moonrise my Paphos, and unimaginable realms of faerie; broad noon shall be my England of the senses and the understanding; the night shall be my Germany of mystic philosophy and dreams.

Not less excellent, except for our less susceptibility in the afternoon, was the charm, last evening, of a January sunset. The western clouds divided and subdivided themselves into pink flakes modulated with tints of unspeakable softness, and the air had so much life and sweetness that it was a pain to come within doors. What was it that nature would say? Was there no meaning in the live repose of the valley behind the mill, and which Homer or Shakespeare could not re-form for me in words? The leafless trees become spires of flame in the sunset, with the blue east for their background, and the stars of the dead calices of flowers, and every withered stem and stubble rimed with frost, contribute something to the mute music.

The inhabitants of cities suppose that the country landscape is pleasant only half the year. I please myself with the graces of the winter scenery, and believe that we are as much touched by it as by the genial influences of summer. To the attentive eye, each moment of the year has its own beauty, and in the same field, it beholds, every hour, a picture which was never seen before, and which shall never be seen again. The heavens change every moment, and reflect their glory or gloom on the plains beneath. The state of the crop in the surrounding farms alters the expression of the earth from week to week. The succession of native plants in the pastures and roadsides, which makes the silent clock by which time tells the summer hours, will make even the divisions of the day sensible to a keen observer. The tribes of birds and insects, like the plants punctual to their time, follow each other, and the year has room for all. By water-courses, the variety is greater. In July, the blue pontederia or pickerel-weed blooms in large beds in the shallow parts of our pleasant river, and swarms with yellow butterflies in continual motion. Art cannot rival this pomp of purple and gold. Indeed the river is a perpetual gala, and boasts each month a new ornament.

But this beauty of Nature which is seen and felt as beauty, is the least part. The shows of day, the dewy morning, the rainbow, mountains, orchards in blossom, stars, moonlight, shadows in still water, and the like, if too eagerly hunted, become shows merely, and mock us with their unreality. Go out of the house to see the moon, and 't is mere tinsel; it will not please as when its light shines upon your necessary journey. The beauty that shimmers in the yellow afternoons of October, who ever could clutch it? Go forth to find it, and it is gone; 't is only a mirage as you look from the windows of diligence.

2. The presence of a higher, namely, of the spiritual element is essential to its perfection. The high and divine beauty which can be loved without effeminacy, is that which is found in combination with the human will. Beauty is the mark God sets upon virtue. Every natural action is graceful. Every heroic act is also decent, and causes the place and the bystanders to shine. We are taught by great actions that the universe is the property of every individual in it. Every rational creature has all nature for his dowry and estate. It is his, if he will. He may divest himself of it; he may creep into a corner, and abdicate his kingdom, as most men do, but he is entitled to the world by his constitution. In proportion to the energy of his thought and will, he takes up the

world into himself. "All those things for which men plough, build, or sail, obey virtue;" said Sallust. "The winds and waves," said Gibbon, "are always on the side of the ablest navigators." So are the sun and moon and all the stars of heaven. When a noble act is done—perchance in a scene of great natural beauty; when Leonidas and his three hundred martyrs consume one day in dying, and the sun and moon come each and look at them once in the steep defile of Thermopylæ; when Arnold Winkelried, in the high Alps, under the shadow of the avalanche, gathers in his side a sheaf of Austrian spears to break the line for his comrades; are not these heroes entitled to add the beauty of the scene to the beauty of the deed? When the bark of Columbus nears the shore of America—before it the beach lined with savages, fleeing out of all their huts of cane; the sea behind; and the purple mountains of the Indian Archipelago around, can we separate the man from the living picture? Does not the New World clothe his form with her palmgroves and savannahs as fit drapery? Ever does natural beauty steal in like air, and envelope great actions. When Sir Harry Vane was dragged up the Towerhill, sitting on a sled, to suffer death as the champion of the English laws, one of the multitude cried out to him, "You never sate on so glorious a seat!" Charles II, to intimidate the citizens of London, caused the patriot Lord Russell to be drawn in an open coach through the principal streets of the city on his way to the scaffold. "But," his biographer says, "the multitude imagined they saw liberty and virtue sitting by his side." In private places, among sordid objects, an act of truth or heroism seems at once to draw to itself the sky as its temple, the sun as its candle. Nature stretches out her arms to embrace man, only let his thoughts be of equal greatness. Willingly does she follow his steps with the rose and the violet, and bend her lines of grandeur and grace to the decoration of her darling child. Only let his thoughts be of equal scope, and the frame will suit the picture. A virtuous man is in unison with her works, and makes the central figure of the visible sphere. Homer, Pindar, Socrates, Phocion, associate themselves fitly in our memory with the geography and climate of Greece. The visible heavens and earth sympathize with Jesus. And in common life whosoever has seen a person of powerful character and happy genius, will have remarked how easily he took all things along with him—the persons, the opinions, and the day, and nature became ancillary to a man.

3. There is still another aspect under which the beauty of the world may be viewed, namely, as it becomes an object of the intellect. Beside the relation of things to virtue, they have a relation to thought. The intellect searches out the absolute order of things as they stand in the mind of God, and without the colors of affection. The intellectual and the active powers seem to succeed each other, and the exclusive activity of the one generates the exclusive activity of the other. There is something unfriendly in each to the other, but they are like the alternate periods of feeding and working in animals; each prepares and will be followed by the other. Therefore does beauty, which, in relation to actions, as we have seen, comes unsought, and comes because it is unsought, remain for the apprehension and pursuit of the intellect; and then again, in its turn, of the active power. Nothing divine dies. All good is eternally reproductive. The beauty of nature re-forms itself in the mind, and not for barren contemplation, but for new creation.

All men are in some degree impressed by the face of the world; some men even to delight. This love of beauty is Taste. Others have the same love in such excess, that, not content with admiring, they seek to embody it in new forms. The creation of beauty is Art.

The production of a work of art throws a light upon the mystery of humanity. A work of art is an abstract or epitome of the world. It is the result or expression of nature, in miniature. For although the works of nature are innumerable and all different, the result or the expression of them all is similar and single. Nature is a sea of forms radically alike and even unique. A leaf, a sunbeam, a landscape, the ocean, make an analogous impression on the mind. What is common to them all—that perfectness and harmony, is beauty. The standard of beauty is the entire circuit of natural forms—the totality of nature; which the Italians expressed by defining beauty "il più nell' uno." Nothing is quite beautiful alone; nothing but is beautiful in the whole. A single object is only so far beautiful as it suggests this universal grace. The poet, the painter, the sculptor, the musician, the architect, seek each to concentrate this radiance of the world on one point, and each in his several work to satisfy the love of beauty which stimulates him to produce. Thus is Art a nature passed through the alembic of man. Thus in art does Nature work through the will of a man filled with the beauty of her first works.

The world thus exists to the soul to satisfy the desire of beauty. This element I call an ultimate end. No reason can be asked or given why the soul seeks beauty. Beauty, in its largest and profoundest sense, is one expression for the universe. God is the all-fair. Truth, and goodness, and beauty, are but different faces of the same All. But beauty in nature is not ultimate. It is the herald of inward and eternal beauty, and is not alone a solid and satisfactory good. It must stand as a part, and not as yet the last or highest expression of the final cause of Nature.

WILD FLOWERS

F. W. BAIN

Hindu mythology finds religious significance in all of nature's phases, from the love of a man and a woman to the blooming of a lotus flower in the wilderness. Here a queen who has eloped with a supposed commoner (really a prince), tells an allegorical story about the lotus. This parable is reprinted from F. W. Bain, A Digit of the Moon, *New York: G. P. Putnam's Sons, 1905.*

Then said Indra: O slender-waisted lady, thou arguest well of the general duty of wives; and yet this does not vindicate thy own infatuation in consorting with such a one as he whom thou has chosen for thy husband. Thou hast sacrificed the flower of thy virgin beauty on an altar unworthy of it, and fallen from the state of a queen to be the wife of a wandering vagabond.

Then said Wanawallarí: O Brahman, every flower, sooner or later, must fade, for this is its destined and inevitable end. Fade it must at last, whether it be on the head of a queen in the palace, or alone in the depths of the wood. And who shall say, whether it is not better for the flower to wither in the wood, than as an ornament in the hair of queens? So then, if I have abandoned my royal position, and betaken myself to the forest and solitude with my husband, what is lost that deserves to be regretted? Art thou so sure in my case that it is a loss and not rather a gain if like a flower I live and fade in the forest alone? For once there was a king who was betrayed by his wife. And he cast off his kingdom like a snake its old skin, and threw away everything like a blade of grass, and turned his back upon the world. And he went, not to the Ganges, but away into the great southern forest, for he said: Let me go where I shall never again see a human face, or hear a human voice again. So day after day he went on into the unknown depths of that terrible forest, till after a time he found himself alone with his shadow among the giant trees. And then, all of a sudden, those trees came abruptly to an end. And he looked, and lo! he stood on the bank of a great river, whose water was studded as far as his eye could see with a countless host of lotus flowers that coloured that region blue. And every lotus had for its lover a great golden bee, that buzzed about it like an incarnation of the sun, come down to earth after self-multiplication, like Krishna among the Gopis, in order that each lotus might think itself alone beloved. And the king marvelled at the sight of that lonely lotus-haunted, bee-booming river, and he lived there till he died, alone. And if the Creator could frame those fair flowers in the midst of that wilderness to live and die with never an eye to see, surely they were better than if they had all been gathered to fade upon the hair of a million queens.

THE FAITH of a NATURALIST

JOHN BURROUGHS

John Burroughs, perhaps the most famous American naturalist, declared his attitude toward God and nature in his book, Accepting the Universe, *Boston: Houghton Mifflin Co., 1920. The chapter on his faith is exceptionally revealing.*

I

To say that man is as good as God would to most persons seem like blasphemy; but to say that man is as good as Nature would disturb no one. Man is a part of Nature, or a phase of Nature, and shares in what we call her imperfections. But what is Nature a part of, or a phase of?—and what or who is its author? Is it not true that this earth which is so familiar to us is as good as yonder morning or evening star and made of the same stuff?—just as much in the heavens, just as truly a celestial abode as it is? Venus seems to us like a great jewel in the crown of night or morning. From Venus the earth would seem like a still larger jewel. The heavens seem afar off and free from all stains and impurities of earth; we lift our eyes and our hearts to them as to the face of the Eternal, but our science reveals no body or place there so suitable for human abode and human happiness as this earth. In fact, this planet is the only desirable heaven of which we have any clue. Innumerable other worlds exist in the abysses of space which may be the abodes of beings superior, and of beings inferior, to ourselves. We place our gods afar off so as to dehumanize them, never suspecting that when we do so we discount their divinity. The more human we are,—remembering that to err is human,—the nearer God we are. Of course good and bad are human concepts and are a verdict upon created things as they stand related to us, promoting or hindering our well-being. In the councils of the Eternal there is apparently no such distinction.

Man is not only as good as God; some men are a good deal better, that is, from our point of view; they attain a degree of excellence of which there is no hint in nature—moral excellence. It is not until we treat man as a part of nature—as a product of the earth as literally as are the trees—that we can reconcile these contradictions. If we could build up a composite man out of all the peoples of the earth, including even the Prussians, he would represent fairly well the God in nature.

Communing with God is communing with our own hearts, our own best selves, not with something foreign and accidental. Saints and devotees have gone into the wilderness to find God; of course they took God with them, and the silence and detachment enabled them to hear the still, small voice of their own souls, as one hears the ticking of his own watch in the stillness of the night. We are not cut off, we are not isolated points; the great currents flow through us and over us and around us, and unite us to the whole of nature. Moses saw God in the burning bush, saw him with the eyes of early man whose divinities were clothed in the extraordinary, the fearful, or the terrible; we see him in the meanest weed that grows, and hear him in the gentle murmur of our own heart's blood. The language of devotion and religious conviction is only the language of soberness and truth written large and aflame with emotion.

Man goes away from home searching for the gods he carries with him always. Man can know and feel and love only man. There is a deal of sound psychology in the new religion called Christian Science—in that part which emphasizes the power of the mind over the body, and the fact that the world is largely what we make it, that evil is only the shadow of good—old truths reburnished. This helps us to understand the hold it has taken upon such a large number of admirable persons. Good and evil are relative terms, but evil is only the shadow of good. Disease is a reality, but not in the same sense that health is a reality. Positive and negative electricity are both facts, but positive and negative good belong to a different order. Christian Science will not keep the distemper out of the house if the sewer-gas gets in; inoculation will do more to prevent typhoid and diphtheria than "declaring the truth" or saying your prayers or counting your beads. In its therapeutical value experimental science is the only safe guide in dealing with human corporal ailments.

We need not fear alienation from God. I feed Him when I feed a beggar. I serve Him when I serve my neighbor. I love Him when I love my friend. I praise Him when I praise the wise and good of any race or time. I shun Him when I shun the leper. I forgive Him when I forgive my enemies. I wound Him when I wound a human being. I forget Him when I forget my duty to others. If I am cruel or unjust or resentful or envious or inhospitable toward any man, woman, or child, I am guilty of all these things toward God: "Inasmuch as ye have done it unto one of the least of these my brethren, ye have done it unto me."

II

I am persuaded that a man without religion falls short of the proper human ideal. Religion, as I use the term, is a spiritual flowering, and the man who has it not is like a plant that never blooms. The mind that does not open and unfold its religious sensibilities in the sunshine of this infinite and spiritual universe, is to be pitied. Men of science do well enough with no other religion than the love of truth, for this is indirectly a love of God. The astronomer, the geologist, the biologist, tracing the footsteps of the Creative Energy throughout the universe—what need has he of any formal, patent-right religion? Were not Darwin, Huxley, Tyndall, and Lyall, and all other seekers and verifiers of natural truth among the most truly religious of men? Any of these men would have gone to hell for the truth—not the truth of creeds and rituals, but the truth as it exists in the councils of the Eternal, and as it is written in the laws of matter and of life.

For my part I had a thousand times rather have Huxley's religion than that of the bishops who sought to discredit him, or Bruno's than that of the church that burnt him. The religion of a man that has no other aim than his own personal safety from some real or imaginary future calamity, is of the selfish, ignoble kind.

Amid the decay of creeds, love of nature has high religious value. This has saved many persons in this world—saved them from mammon-worship, and from the frivolity and insincerity of the crowd. It has made their lives placid and sweet. It has given them an inexhaustible field for inquiry, for enjoyment, for the exercise of all their powers, and in the end has not left them soured and dissatisfied. It has made them contented and at home wherever they are in nature—in the house not made with hands. This house is their church, and the rocks and the hills are the altars, and the creed is written in the leaves of the trees and in the flowers of the field and in the sands of the shore. A new creed every day and new preachers, and holy days all the week through. Every walk to the woods is a religious rite, every bath in the stream is a saving ordinance. Communion service is at all hours, and the bread and wine are from the heart and marrow of Mother Earth. There are no heretics in Nature's church; all are believers, all are communicants. The beauty of natural religion is that you have it all the time; you do not have to seek it afar off in myths and legends, in catacombs, in garbled texts, in miracles of dead saints or wine-bibbing friars. It is of to-day; it is now and here; it is everywhere. The crickets chirp it, the birds sing it, the breezes chant it, the thunder proclaims it, the streams murmur it, the unaffected man lives it. Its incense rises from the plowed fields, it is on the morning breeze, it is in the forest breath and in the spray of the wave. The frosts write it in exquisite characters, the dews impearl it, and the rainbow paints it on the cloud. It is not an insurance policy underwritten by a bishop or a priest; it is not even a faith; it is a love, an enthusiasm, a consecration to natural truth.

The God of sunshine and of storms speaks a less equivocal language than the God of revelation.

Our fathers had their religion and their fathers had theirs, but they were not ours, and could not be in those days and under those conditions. But their religions lifted them above themselves; they healed their wounds; they consoled them for many of the failures and disappointments of this world; they developed character; they tempered the steel in their nature. How childish to us seems the plan of salvation, as our fathers found it in the fervid and, I freely say, inspired utterances of Saint Paul! But it saved them, it built character, it made life serious, it was an heroic creed which has lost credence in our more knowing and more frivolous age. We see how impossible it is, but we do not see the great natural truths upon which it rests.

A man is not saved by the truth of the things he believes, but by the truth of his belief—its sincerity, its harmony with his character. The absurdities of the popular religions do not matter;

what matters is the lukewarm belief, the empty forms, the shallow conceptions of life and duty. We are prone to think that if the creed is false, the religion is false. Religion is an emotion, an inspiration, a feeling of the Infinite, and may have its root in any creed or in no creed. What can be more unphilosophical than the doctrines of the Christian Scientists? Yet Christian Science is a good practical religion. It makes people cheerful, happy, and helpful—yes, and helps make them healthy too. Its keynote is love, and love holds the universe together. Any creed that ennobles character and opens a door or a window upon the deeper meanings of this marvelous universe is good enough to live by, and good enough to die by. The Japanese-Chinese religion of ancestor worship, sincerely and devoutly held, is better than the veneer of much of our fashionable well-dressed religion.

Guided by appearances alone, how surely we should come to look upon the sun as a mere appendage of the earth!—as much so as is the moon. How near it seems at sunrise and sunset, and as if these phenomena directly involved the sun, extending to it and modifying its light and heat! We do not realize that these are merely terrestrial phenomena, and that the sun, so to speak, knows them not.

Viewed from the sun the earth is a mere speck in the sky, and the amount of the total light and heat from the sun that is received on the earth is so small that the mind can hardly grasp it. Yet for all practical purposes the sun shines for us alone. Our relation to it could not be any more direct and sustaining if it were created for that purpose. It is immanent in the life of the globe. It is the source of all our energy and therefore of our life. Its bounties are universal. The other planets find it is their sun also. It is as special and private to them as to us. We think the sun paints the bow on the cloud, but the bow follows from the laws of optics. The sun knows it not.

It is the same with what we call God. His bounty is of the same universal, impersonal kind, and yet for all practical purposes it exists especially for us, it is immanent every moment in our lives. There is no special Providence. Nature sends the rain upon the just and the unjust, upon the sea as upon the land. We are here and find life good because Providence is general and not special. The conditions are not too easy, the struggle has made men of us. The bitter has tempered the sweet. Evil has put us on our guard and keeps us so. We pay for what we get.

III

That wise old Roman, Marcus Aurelius, says, "Nothing is evil which is according to nature." At that moment he is thinking especially of death which, when it comes in the course of nature, is not an evil, unless life itself is also an evil. After the lamp of life is burned out, death is not an evil, rather is it a good. But premature death, death by accident or disease, before a man has done his work or used up his capital of vitality, is an evil. Disease itself is an evil, but if we lived according to nature there would be no disease; we should die the natural, painless death of old age. Of course there is no such thing as absolute evil or absolute good. Evil is that which is against our well-being, and good is that which promotes it. We always postulate the existence of life when we speak of good and evil. Excesses in nature are evil to us because they bring destruction and death in their train. They are disharmonies in the scheme of things, because they frustrate and bring to naught. The war which Marcus Aurelius was waging when he wrote those passages was an evil in itself, though good might come out of it.

Everything in organic nature—trees, grasses, flowers, insects, fishes, mammals—is beset by evil of some kind. The natural order is good because it brought us here and keeps us here, but evil has always dogged our footsteps. Leaf-blight is an evil to the tree, smallpox is an evil to man, frost is an evil to the insects, flood an evil to the fishes.

Moral evil—hatred, envy, greed, lying, cruelty, cheating—is of another order. These vices have no existence below the human sphere. We call them evils because they are disharmonies; they are inimical to the highest standard of human happiness and well-being. They make a man less a man, they work discord and develop needless friction. Sand in the engine of your car and water in the gasoline are evils, and malice and jealousy and selfishness in your heart are analogous evils.

In our day we read the problem of Nature and God in a new light, the light of science, or of emancipated human reason, and the old myths mean little to us. We accept Nature as we find it, and do not crave the intervention of a God that sits behind and is superior to it. The self-activity of the cosmos suffices. We accept the tornadoes and earthquakes and world wars, and do not lose faith. We arm ourselves against them as best we can. We accept the bounty of the rain, the sunshine, the soil, the changing seasons, and the vast armory of non-living forces, and from them equip or teach ourselves to escape, endure, modify, or ward off the destructive and non-human forces that beset our way. We draw our strength from the Nature that seems and is so regardless of us; our health and wholeness are its gifts. The biologic ages, with all their carnival of huge and monstrous forms, had our well-being at heart. The evils and dangers that beset our way have been outmatched by the good and the helpful. The deep-sea fish would burst and die if brought to the surface; the surface life would be crushed and killed in the deep sea. Life adapts itself to its environment; hard conditions make it hard. Winds, floods, inclement seasons, have driven it around the earth; the severer the cold, the thicker the fur; compensations always abound. If Nature is not all-wise and all-merciful from our human point of view, she has placed us in a world where our own wisdom and mercy can be developed; she has sent us to a school in which we learn to see her own shortcomings and imperfections, and to profit by them.

The unreasoning, unforeseeing animals suffer more from the accidents of nature—drought, flood, lightning—than man does; but man suffers more from evils of his own making—war, greed, intemperance, pestilence—so that the development in both lines goes on, and life is still at the flood.

Good and evil are inseparable. We cannot have light without shade, or warmth without cold, or life without death, or development without struggle. The struggle for life, of which Darwinism makes so much, is only the struggle of the chick to get out of the shell, or of the flower to burst its bud, or of the root to penetrate the soil. It is not the struggle of battle and hate—the justification of war and usurpation—it is for the most part a beneficent struggle with the environment, in which the fittest of the individual units of a species survive, but in which the strong and the feeble, the great and the small of species alike survive. The lamb survives with the lion, the wren with the eagle, the Esquimo with the European—all manner of small and delicate forms survive with the great and robust. One species of carnivora, or of rodents, or herbivora, does not, as a rule, exterminate another species. It is true that species prey upon species, that cats eat mice, that hawks eat smaller birds, and that man slays and eats the domestic animals. Probably man alone has exterminated species. But outside of man's doings all the rest belongs to Nature's system of checks and balances, and bears no analogy to human or inhuman wars and conquests.

Life struggles with matter, the tree struggles with the wind and with other trees. Man struggles with gravity, cold, wet, heat, and all the forces that hinder him. The tiniest plant that grows has to force its root down into the soil; earlier than that it has to burst its shell or case. The corn struggles to lift itself up after the storm has beaten it down; effort, effort, everywhere in the organic world. Says Whitman:

> "Urge and urge and urge,
> Always the procreant urge of the world."

IV

Every few years we have an ice-storm or a snowstorm that breaks down and disfigures the trees. Some trees suffer much more than others. The storm goes its way; the laws of physical force prevail; the great world of mechanical forces is let loose upon the small world of vital forces; occasionally a tree is so crushed that it never entirely recovers; but after many years the woods and groves have repaired the damages and taken on their wonted thrifty appearance. The evil was only temporary; the world of trees has suffered no permanent setback. But had the trees been conscious beings, what a deal of suffering they would have experienced! An analogous visitation to human communities entails a heritage of misery, but in time it too is forgotten and its scars healed. Fire, flood, war, epidemics, earthquakes, are such visitations, but the race survives them and reaps good from them.

We say that Nature cares nothing for the individual, but only for the race or the species. The whole organic world is at war with the inorganic, and as in human wars the individuals are sacrificed that the army, the whole, may live; so in the strife and competition of nature, the separate units fall that the mass may prosper.

It is probably true that in the course of the biological history of the earth, whole species have been rendered extinct by parasites, or by changing outward conditions. But this has been the exception, and not the rule. The chestnut blight now seems to threaten the very existence of this species of tree in this country, but I think the chances are that this fungus will meet with some natural check.

In early summer comes the June drop of apples. The trees start with more fruit than they can carry, and if they are in vigorous health, they will drop the surplus. It is a striking illustration of Nature's methods. The tree does its own thinning. But if not at the top of its condition, it fails to do this. It takes health and strength simply to let go; only a living tree drops its fruit or its leaves; only a growing man drops his outgrown opinions.

If we put ourselves in the place of the dropped apples, we must look upon our fate as unmixed evil. If we put ourselves in the place of the tree and of the apples that remain on it, the June drop would appear an unmixed good—finer fruit, and a healthier, longer-lived tree results. Nature does not work so much to specific as to universal ends. The individual may go, but the type must remain. The ranks may be decimated, but the army and its cause must triumph. Life in all its forms is a warfare only in the sense that it is a struggle with its outward conditions, in which, other things being equal, the strongest force prevails. Small and weak forms prevail also, because the competing forms are small and weak, or because at the feast of life there is a place for the small and weak also. But lion against lion, man against man, mouse against mouse, the strongest will, in the end, be the victor.

Man's effort is to save waste, to reduce friction, to take short cuts, to make smooth the way, to seize the advantage, to economize time, but the physical forces know none of these things.

Go into the woods and behold the evil the trees have to contend with—all typical of the evil we have to contend with—too crowded in places, one tree crushing another by its fall, specimens on every hand whose term of life might be lengthened by a little wise surgery; borers, blight, disease, insect pests, storm, wreckage, thunderbolt scars, or destruction—evil in a hundred forms besetting every tree, and sooner or later leaving its mark. A few escape—oaks, maples, pines, elms—and reach a greater age than the others, but they fail at last, and when they have rounded out their green century, or ten centuries, and go down in a gale, or in the stillness of a summer night, how often younger trees are marred or crushed by their fall! But come back after many long years, and their places are filled, and all the scars are healed. The new generation of trees is feeding upon the accumulations of the old. Evil is turned to good. The destruction of the cyclone, the ravages of fire, the wreckage of the ice-storm, are all obliterated and the forest-spirit is rank and full again.

There is no wholesale exemption from this rule of waste and struggle in this world, nor probably in any other. We have life on these terms. The organic world develops under pressure from within and from without. Rain brings the perils of rain, fire brings the perils of fire, power brings the perils of power. The great laws go our way, but they will break us or rend us if we fail to keep step with them. Unmixed good is a dream; unmixed happiness is a dream; perfection is a dream; heaven and hell are both dreams of our mixed and struggling lives, the one the outcome of our aspirations for the good, the other the outcome of our fear of evil.

The trees in the woods, the plants in the fields encounter hostile forces the year through; storms crash or overthrow them; visible and invisible enemies prey upon them; yet are the fields clothed in verdure and the hills and plains mantled with superb forests. Nature's haphazard planting and sowing and her wasteful weeding and trimming do not result in failure as these methods do with us. A failure of hers with one form or species results in the success of some other form. All successes are hers. Allow time enough and the forest returns in the path of the tornado, but maybe with other species of trees. The birds and squirrels plant oaks and chestnuts amid the pines and the winds plant pines amid the oaks and chestnuts. The robins and the cedar-birds sow the red cedar broadcast over the landscape, and plant the Virginia creeper and the poison-ivy by every stub and fence-post. The poison-ivy is a triumph of Nature as truly as is the grapevine or the morning-glory. All are hers. Man specializes; he selects this or that, selects the wheat and rejects the tares; but Nature generalizes; she has the artist's disinterestedness; all is good; all are parts of her scheme. She nourishes the foul-smelling cat-brier as carefully as she does the rose. Each creature, with man at the head, says, "The world is mine; it was created for me." Evidently it was created for all, at least all forms are at home here. Nature's system of checks and balances preserves her working equilibrium. If a species of forest worm under some exceptionally favoring conditions gets such a start that it threatens to destroy our beech and maple forests, presently a parasite, stimulated by this turn in its favor, appears and restores the balance. For two or three seasons the beech-woods in my native town were ravaged by some kind of worm or beetle; in midsummer the sunlight came into them as if the roof had been taken off; later they swarmed with white millers. But the scourge was suddenly checked—some parasite, probably a species of ichneumon-fly, was on hand to curtail the dangerous excess.

I am only trying to say that after we have painted Nature as black as the case will allow, after we have depicted her as a savage beast, a devastating storm, a scorching desert, a consuming fire, an all-engulfing earthquake, or as war, pestilence, famine, we have only depicted her from our limited human point of view. But even from that point of view the favoring conditions of life are so many, living bodies are so adaptive, the lift of the evolutionary impulse is so unconquerable, the elemental laws and forces are so overwhelmingly on our side, that our position in the universe is still an enviable one. "Though he slay me, yet will I trust in him." Slain, I shall nourish some other form of life, and the books will still balance—not my books, but the vast ledgers of the Eternal.

In the old times we accounted for creation in the simple terms of the Hebrew Scriptures—"In the beginning God created the heaven and the earth." We even saw no discrepancy in the tradition that creation took place in the spring. But when we attempt to account for creation in the terms of science or naturalism, the problem is far from being so simple. We have not so tangible a point from which to start. It is as if we were trying to find the end or the beginning of the circle. Round and round we go, caught in the endless and beginningless currents of the Creative Energy; no fixity or finality anywhere; rest and motion, great and small, up and down, heat and cold, good and evil, near and far, only relative; cause and effect merging and losing themselves in each other; life and death perpetually playing into each other's hands; interior within interior; depth beneath depth; height above height; the tangible thrilled and vibrating with the intangible; the material in bonds to the non-material; invisible, impalpable forces streaming around us and through us; perpetual change and transformation on every hand; every day a day of creation, every night a revelation of unspeakable grandeur; suns and systems forming in the cyclones of stardust; the whole starry host of heaven flowing like a meadow brook, but where, or whence, who can tell? The center everywhere, the circumference nowhere; pain and pleasure, good and evil, inextricably mixed; the fall of man a daily and hourly occurrence; the redemption of man, the same! Heaven or hell waiting by every doorstep, boundless, beginningless, unspeakable, immeasurable—what wonder that we seek a short cut through this wilderness and appeal to the supernatural?

When I look forth upon the world and see how, regardless of man and his well-being, the operations of Nature go on—how the winds and the storms wreck him or destroy him, how the drought or the floods bring to naught his industries, how not the least force in heaven or earth turns aside for him, or makes any exception to him; in short, how all forms of life are perpetually ground between the upper and the nether millstones of the contending and clashing natural material forces, I ask myself: "Is there nothing, then, under the sun, or beyond the sun, that has a stake in our well-being? Is life purely a game of chance, and is it all luck that we are here in a world so richly endowed to meet all our requirements?" Serene Reason answers: "No, it is not luck as in a lottery. It is the good fortune of the whole. It was inherent in the constitution of the whole, and it continues because of its adaptability; life is here because it fits itself into the scheme of things; it is flexible and compromising." We find the world good to be in because we are adapted to it, and not it to us. The vegetable growth upon the rocks where the sea is forever pounding is a type of life; the waves favor its development. Life takes advantage of turbulence as well as of quietude, of drought as well as of floods, of deserts as well as of marshes, of the sea-bottom as well as of the mountain-tops. Both animal and vegetable life trim their sails to the forces that beat upon them. The image of the sail is a good one. Life avails itself of the half-contrary winds; it captures and imprisons their push in its sails; by yielding a little, it makes headway in the teeth of the gale; it gives and takes; without struggle, without opposition, life would not be life. The sands of the shore do not struggle with the waves, nor the waves with the sands; the buffeting ends where it began. But trees struggle with the wind, fish struggle with the flood, man struggles with his environment; all draw energy from the forces that oppose them. Life gains as it spends; its waste is an investment. Not so with purely material bodies. They are like the clock, they must be perpetually wound from without. A living body is a clock, perpetually self-wound from within.

The faith and composure of the naturalist or naturist are proof against the worst that Nature can do. He sees the cosmic forces only; he sees nothing directly mindful of man, but man himself;

he sees the intelligence and beneficence of the universe flowering in man; he sees life as a mysterious issue of the warring element; he sees human consciousness and our sense of right and wrong, of truth and justice, as arising in the evolutionary sequence, and turning and sitting in judgment upon all things; he sees that there can be no life without pain and death; that there can be no harmony without discord; that opposites go hand in hand; that good and evil are inextricably mingled; that the sun and blue sky are still there behind the clouds, unmindful of them; that all is right with the world if we extend our vision deep enough; that the ways of Nature are the ways of God if we do not make God in our own image, and make our comfort and well-being the prime object of Nature. Our comfort and well-being are provided for in the constitution of the world, but we may say that they are not guaranteed; they are contingent upon many things, but the chances are upon our side. He that would save his life shall lose it—lose it in forgetting that the universe is not a close corporation, or a patented article, and that it exists for other ends than our own. But he who can lose his life in the larger life of the whole shall save it in a deeper, truer sense.